Constellations

DOT-TO-DOT

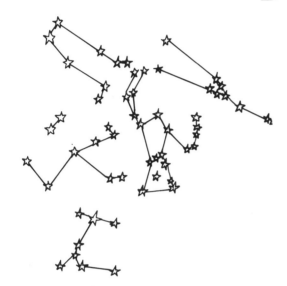

Evan and Lael Kimble

Illustrated by Richard Salvucci

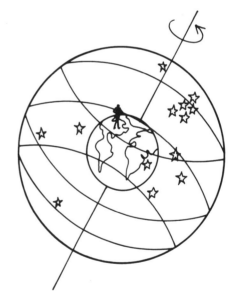

Sterling Publishing Co., Inc.

New York

For Declan and Susanna

The following books were essential in the writing of this book, and are full of additional information for anyone interested in the stars:
Patterns in the Sky, by Julius D.W. Staal,
365 Starry Nights, by Chet Raymo,
Constellation Guidebook, by Antonin Rukl,
National Audubon Society Field Guide to the Night Sky, Mark R. Chartrand

10   9   8   7   6   5   4   3   2

Published by Sterling Publishing Company, Inc.
387 Park Avenue South, New York, N.Y. 10016
© 2001 by Evan and Lael Kimble
Distributed in Canada by Sterling Publishing
C/o Canadian Manda Group, One Atlantic Avenue, Suite 105
Toronto, Ontario, Canada M6K 3E7
Distributed in Great Britain and Europe by Chris Lloyd at Orca Book
Services, Stanley House, Fleets Lane, Poole BH15 3AJ, England.
Distributed in Australia by Capricorn Link (Australia) Pty. Ltd.
P.O. Box 704, Windsor, NSW 2756 Australia

Printed in China

Sterling ISBN 0-8069-2397-0

CONTENTS

CASSIOPEIA, THE QUEEN

Legend: Cassiopeia was the queen of an ancient land. She boasted that she and her daughter were more beautiful than the water nymphs. She bragged so much that she made the gods angry, especially Poseidon, god of the sea. He created a terrible sea-monster called Cetus to attack the people of her country.

Number of Stars: 5

Special Stars: Tycho's star, an exploded star called a "supernova," was named for the astronomer Tycho Brahe, who discovered it in 1572. All five stars are bright and they form a W shape. This constellation is very easy to see. It also helps you find which way is north. It lies on one side of the North Star, and the Big Dipper is on the other.

Did You Know? Different cultures see other images in the sky. Most of the ones we know come from Greek and Roman mythology, but other people from other places and times saw different things in the stars.

• This constellation is sometimes called Cassiopeia's Chair.

• The Celtic people of Britain saw it as the home of the King of the Fairies.

Arabs saw Cassiopeia as a woman's hand painted with henna, a vegetable dye Arab women use to tattoo their hands.

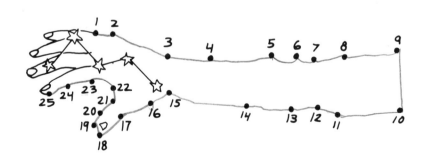

4

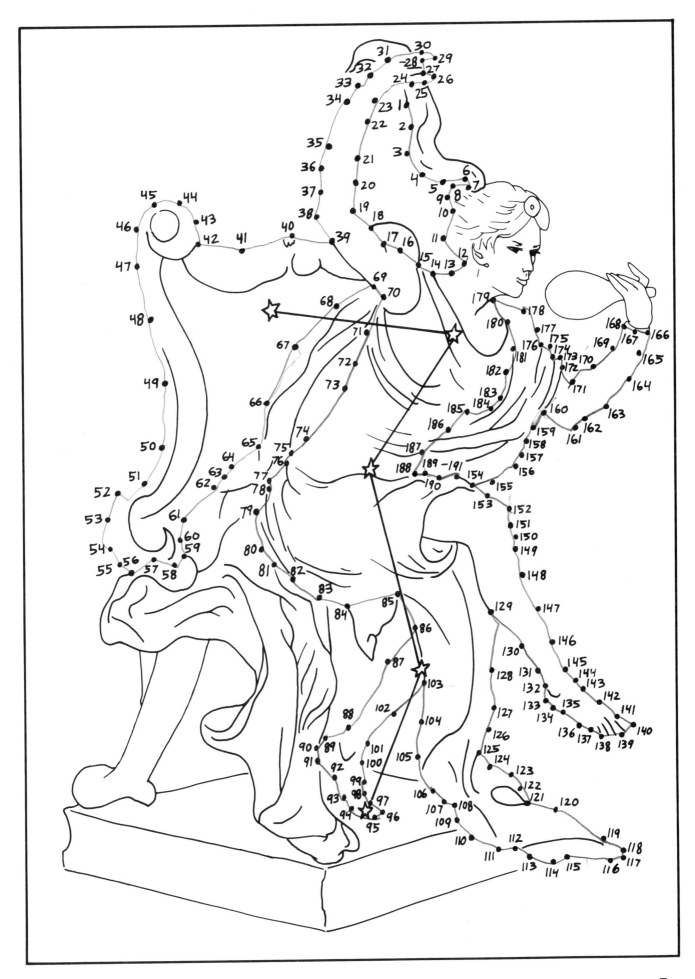

CEPHEUS, the King

Legend: Cepheus was the king who was married to Cassiopeia. Cetus, the sea-monster, was attacking his country, so he went to consult the oracle to find out what to do. The oracle told him that if he gave his daughter Princess Andromeda to the monster, Poseidon would forgive them all and the attacks would end.

Number of Stars: 9

Special Stars: One of the most beautiful double stars (two stars that are so close together that they look like one) are in this constellation—Delta Cephei, and Erakis, a red-orange star.

Did You Know? Almost all the points of light we see in the sky, including the sun, Earth, and all the planets, are in a huge group called the Milky Way Galaxy. Part of the Milky Way Galaxy is a bright ribbon of stars across the sky. It is the part with the most stars in it.

The Milky Way Galaxy is shaped like a spiral.

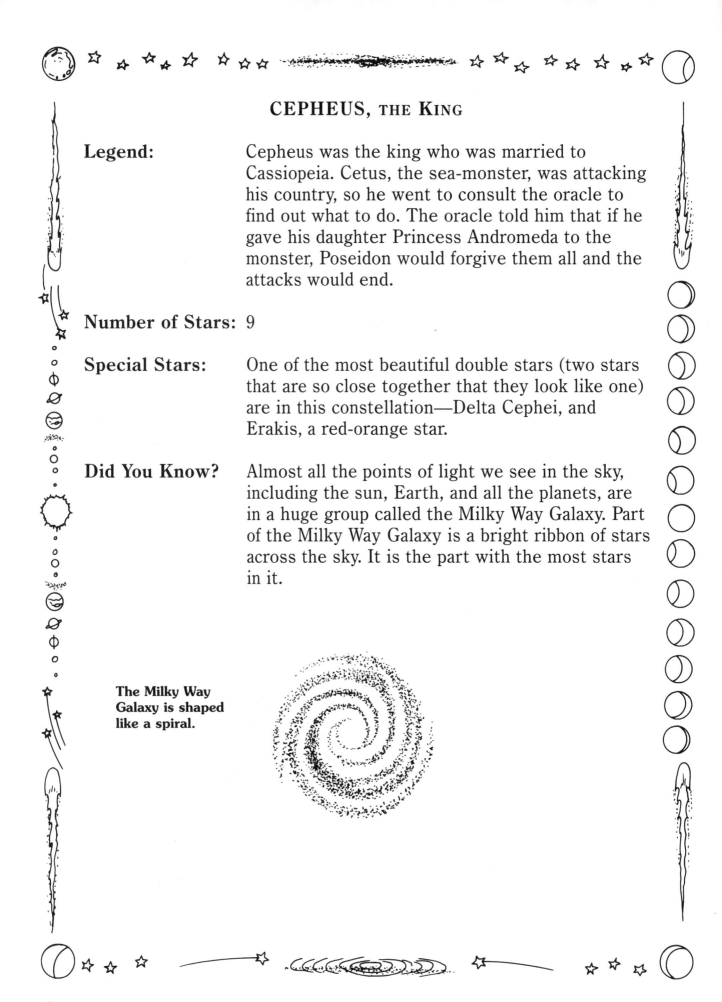

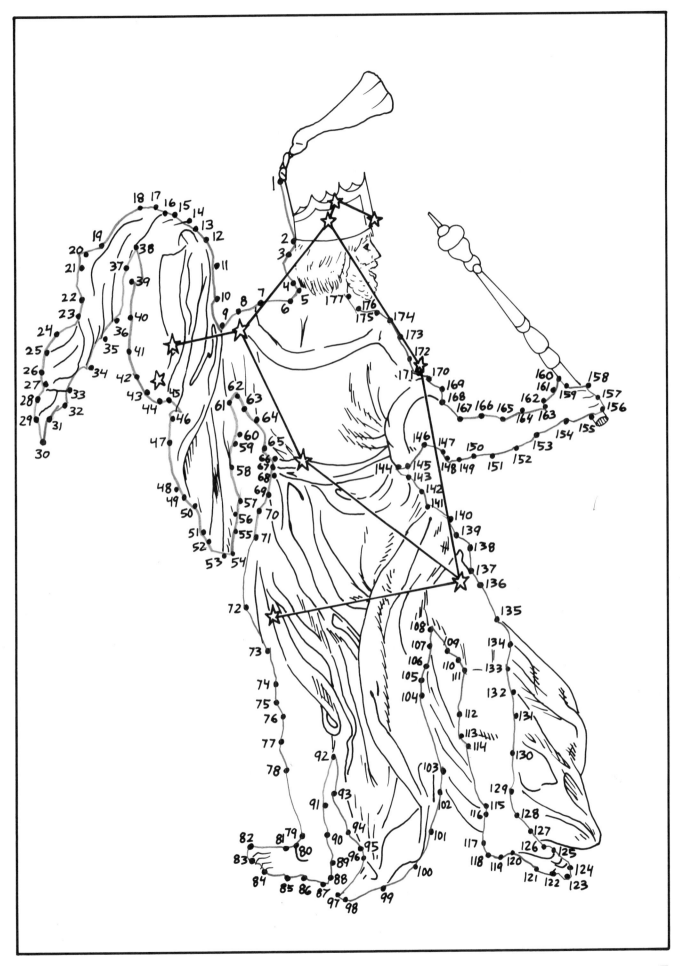

ANDROMEDA, THE PRINCESS

Legend: The beautiful daughter of Cassiopeia and Cepheus, Andromeda was chained to a rock by the sea so that she could be sacrificed to the sea-monster that Poseidon created. Through this sacrifice, the people of the country would be saved. Perseus, the hero, was passing by and saw her in danger. Just in time he rescued her and destroyed the monster. Later, he and Andromeda were married.

Number of Stars: 8

Special Stars: The Andromeda Galaxy is a small hazy spot at her knee. It contains billions of stars and is three million light years away. Even though that is very far away, it is still the closest galaxy to our own galaxy, the Milky Way.

Did You Know? The Andromeda Galaxy is bigger than our galaxy, the Milky Way. You don't need a telescope to see it. You can see it well with binoculars and a dark sky.

The Andromeda Galaxy has an oval shape.

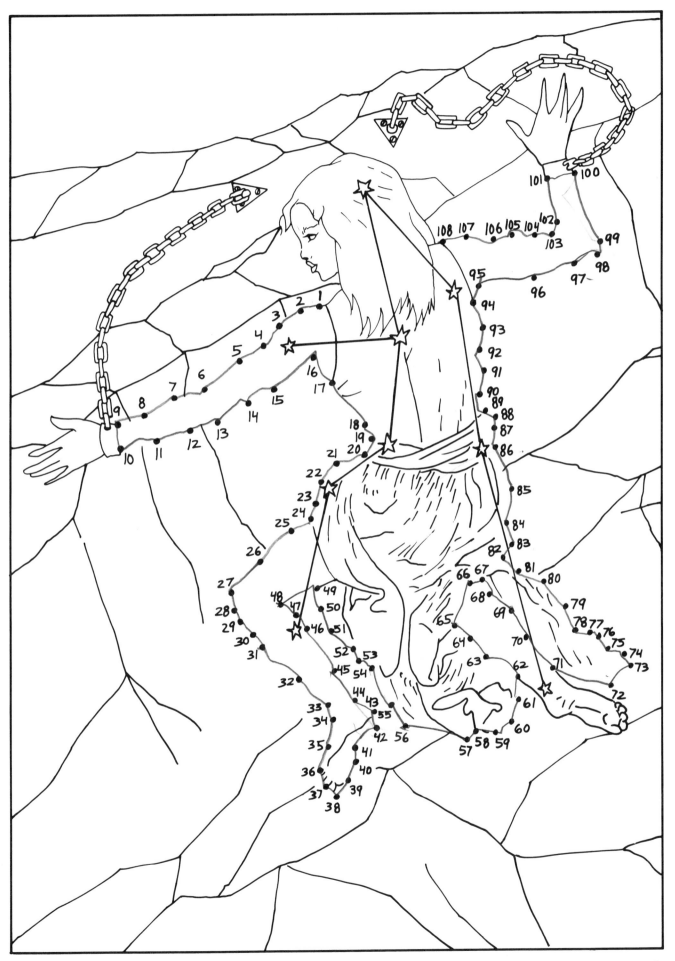

9

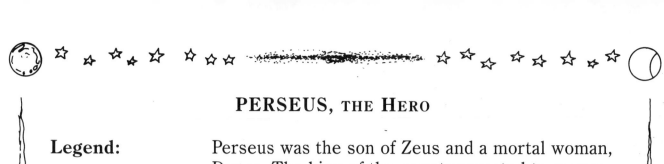

PERSEUS, THE HERO

Legend:

Perseus was the son of Zeus and a mortal woman, Danae. The king of the country wanted to marry his mother, and Perseus agreed to do anything the king wanted if he would only leave Danae alone. The king figured that this was his chance to get rid of Perseus, so he asked for the head of Medusa, the Gorgon. She was a terrifying monster with snakes for hair, and she was so ugly that anyone who looked at her was turned to stone. Perseus prayed to Athena for help, and with her assistance flew to where Medusa lived. To keep from being turned to stone, he looked at Medusa's reflection in his shield and chopped off her head. While on his way home with Medusa's head, he rescued Andromeda from Cetus, the sea-monster.

Number of Stars: 17

Special Stars:

Algenib, a yellow supergiant, and the bright red Algol, the "Demon Star," is also known as Medusa's "eye."

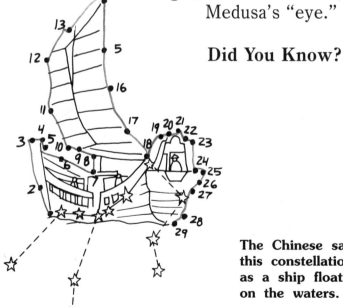

Did You Know? A meteor shower takes place each year around August 10–12 in this part of the sky. Meteors are bits of rock and dust in space that burn up like fireworks when they get too close to Earth.

The Chinese saw this constellation as a ship floating on the waters.

PEGASUS, THE WINGED HORSE

Legend: Pegasus was created when Perseus killed Medusa. Some drops of her blood fell onto the ocean waves, and the winged horse was born. He was a fun-loving animal, and flew back and forth between Olympus, the land of the gods, and Earth. A young man named Bellerophon captured him and, with his help, killed the dreadful Chimera, a fire-breathing monster.

Number of Stars: 14

Special Stars: The stars forming the body of the horse make up "The Great Square of Pegasus."

Close to Pegasus' nose is a cluster of stars that looks like a misty puff of breath coming from the great horse. You need a telescope to see it well. This group, called a "globular cluster," lies outside of our Milky Way Galaxy.

• Long before the Greek legends, this constellation was seen as a horse by the people of Mesopotamia.

• In another legend, Perseus was riding Pegasus when he rescued Andromeda from the sea-monster Cetus.

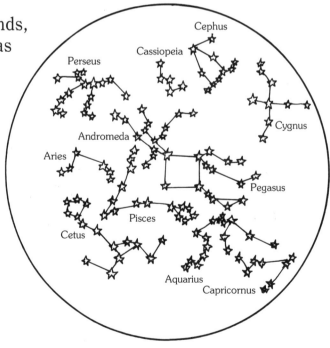

Major Constellations of the Autumn Sky

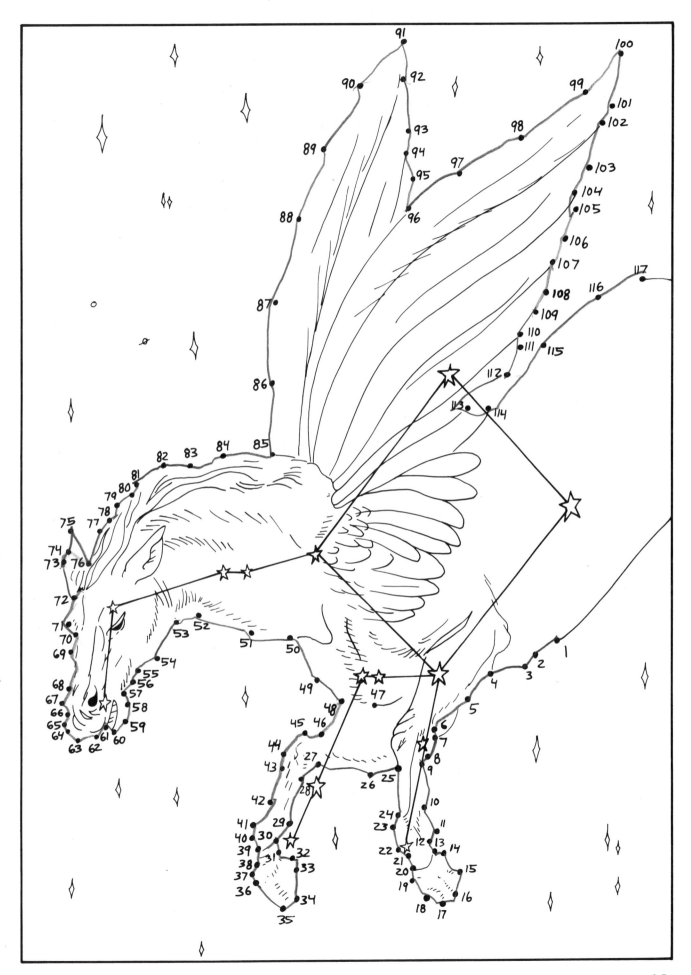

13

CETUS, the Sea-Monster

Legend: Cetus, the sea-monster, was sent by Poseidon, god of the sea, to attack the coast of Greece. It caused so much trouble that Cepheus, the king, chained his daughter Andromeda to a rock as an offering to the monster to make him stop. Perseus the hero saved Andromeda. Some legends say he did it by showing the head of Medusa so that Cetus turned to stone and sank.

Number of Stars: 17

Special Stars: A star called Mira (which means "wonderful" in Latin), is in the neck of Cetus. It changes in brightness. For five months, it is so dim that it is invisible to the eye, then for the next six months, it gets brighter and brighter, before fading again.

Star Facts: If you lived in Greece, you would never see Cetus' body rise above the horizon. If you were looking out over the Mediterranean Sea, it would look as if the monster were raising its head out of the water.

• Natives of northern Brazil saw Cetus as a jaguar, and the jaguar for them was the god of storms and hurricanes.

• The Chinese saw the head of Cetus as a white tiger.

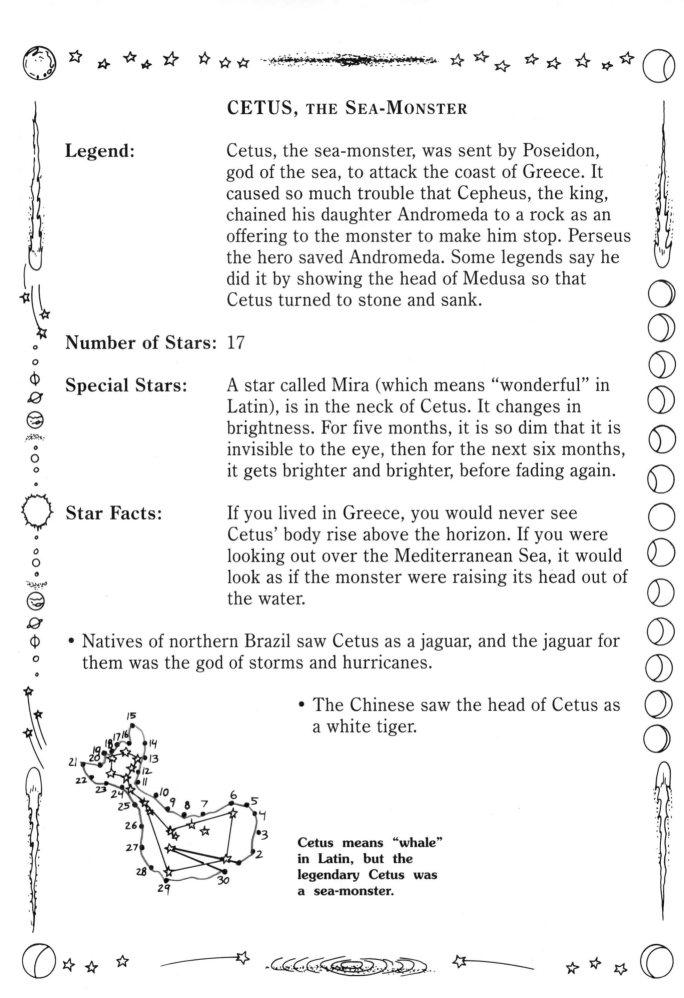

Cetus means "whale" in Latin, but the legendary Cetus was a sea-monster.

15

AQUARIUS, THE WATER-CARRIER

Legend: Aquarius carried drinking water to the gods in a great cup. Zeus always liked to have Aquarius by his side. There are stories in many old cultures about a great flood. Some of them say that it was Aquarius who poured out the water that flooded the world.

Number of Stars: 16

Star Facts: Twelve constellations in the sky make up the zodiac. Each month, the sun passes through a different one. They form a ring around the middle of the sky called the Ecliptic. Aquarius is one of the twelve signs of the zodiac. The others are the Ram, the Bull, the Twins, the Crab, the Lion, the Maiden, the Scales, the Scorpion, the Archer, the Sea-Goat, and the Fish.

Did You Know? Comets are big balls of dust and ice. They zoom around the sun. When they get closer to the sun, the heat makes them melt a little bit. Then long tails of gas stream out from behind the comets.

• The Egyptians thought of this constellation as Khnum, the god who brought water to the land.

• This constellation was the first sign of the old Chinese zodiac, the Rat, bringer of water.

As comets approach the sun their tails get longer.

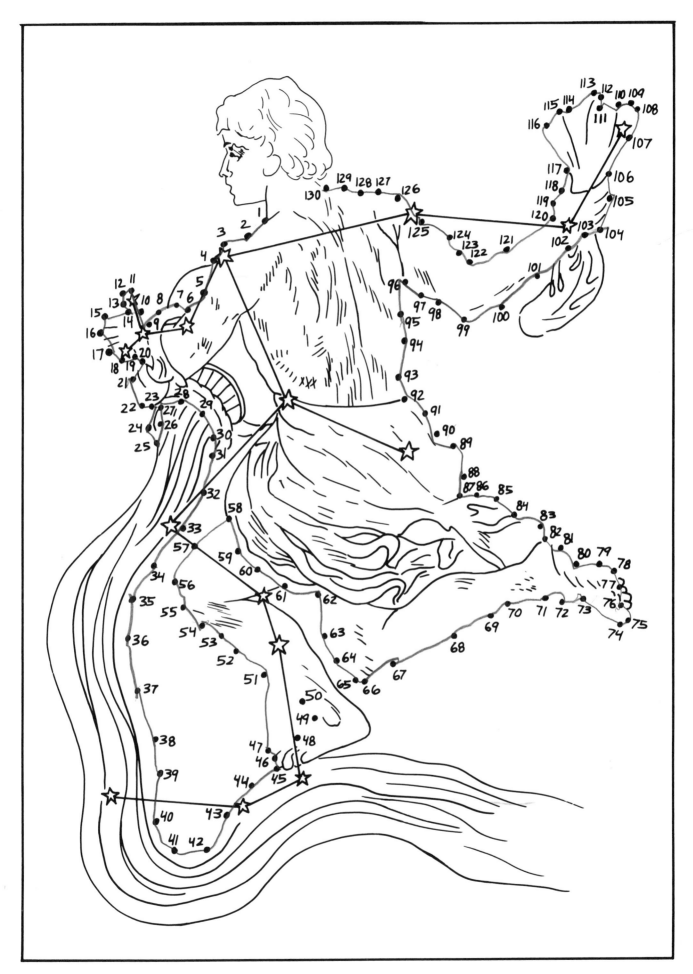

PISCES, the Fish

Legend: In Greek mythology, the goddess Aphrodite and her son Eros were surprised by Typhon, a terrifying monster. Typhon could live in flames but not in water. Aphrodite had been born from the foam of the sea, so she could escape through water. She and Eros turned themselves into fish, tied their tails together so they would not get separated, and swam deep into the sea. This moment is shown in the constellation of Pisces.

Number of Stars: 19

Special Stars: One of the smallest known stars, Van Maanen's Star, is in Pisces. It is called a "white dwarf," which means it is a small, cool star. The star's name, Alrisha, means "the Knot" and the star is the spot where the two fish are tied together.

Star Facts: Pisces is one of the constellations in the zodiac. In the Chinese zodiac this constellation is the Pig.

Did You Know? In the year 7 B.C.E., the planets Jupiter and Saturn were in the exact same place in the sky, together with some other stars in Pisces. When planets are in the same place in the sky, it is called a conjunction. This conjunction may have shone very brightly, and might be the scientific explanation for the Star of Bethlehem.

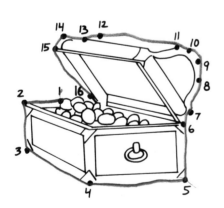

The Greeks thought of fish as powerful creatures who have incredible wealth hidden away.

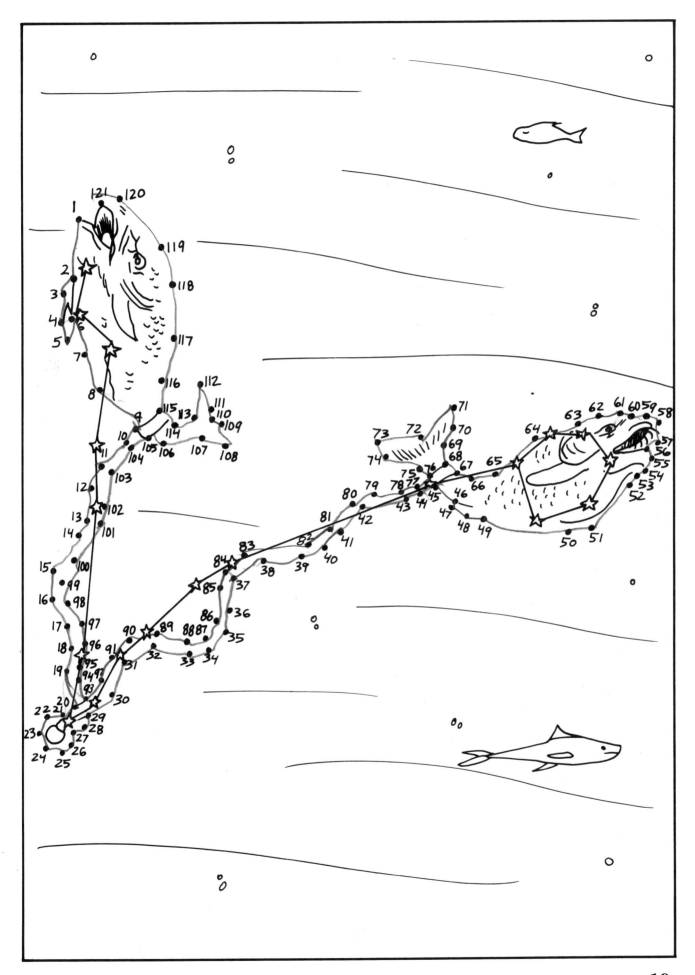

ARIES, THE RAM

Legend: There are many stories about rams. One, from Greek myth, tells how a ram saved the life of Odysseus, a great hero and warrior. Odysseus and his men had been captured by a giant called Cyclops, who held them in a cave and ate two of them each day. Odysseus and his men hid underneath the rams that Cyclops also kept in the cave. When the giant let out the rams to graze in the fields, the warriors escaped.

Another myth tells of a magical ram that Mercury created, with golden fleece. The ram was sacrificed to Jupiter and its fleece was guarded by a dragon. Jason and the members of his expedition went after the Golden Fleece and had many adventures before he finally captured it.

Number of Stars: 6

Star Facts: Aries is one of the constellations in the zodiac. In the Chinese zodiac this constellation is the Dog.

Did You Know? In ancient times, on the first day of spring the sun crossed the point in the sky where Aries appears. However, because Earth wobbles a little on its axis over thousands of years, the sun now lands on Pisces on the first day of spring.

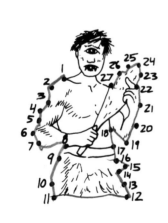

Cyclops had only one eye.

PHOENIX, THE MAGICAL BIRD

Legend: The Phoenix is a mythical bird that was said to live for 500 years. At the end of its life, it would build a nest, and when the sun was highest in the sky, the nest would catch fire and the bird would burn up. But from the ashes, a worm would crawl out, and the sun's heat would turn it into a new Phoenix. In this way, the Phoenix stands for things that may change or fade, but never die.

Number of Stars: 9 (Two are double stars, so they look like single stars to us.)

Star Facts: Phoenix is seen only from the southern hemisphere.

Did You Know? Each year Earth travels around the sun one time. Because Earth is moving, we see different parts of the night sky during different times of the year. That's why some constellations are best seen in summer, and some are only visible in winter.

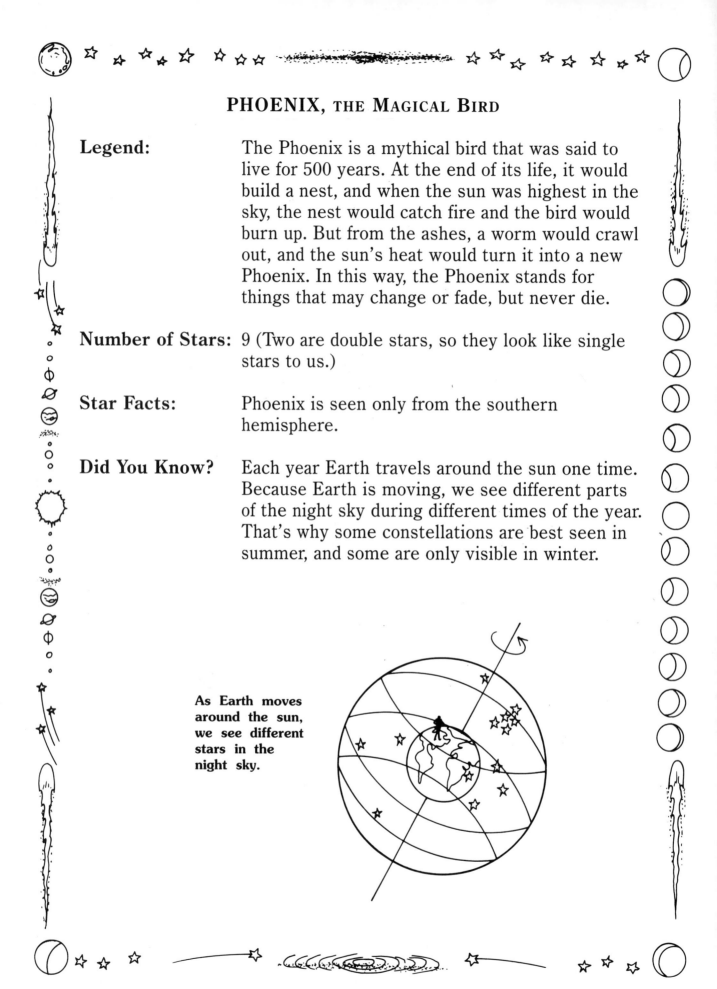

As Earth moves around the sun, we see different stars in the night sky.

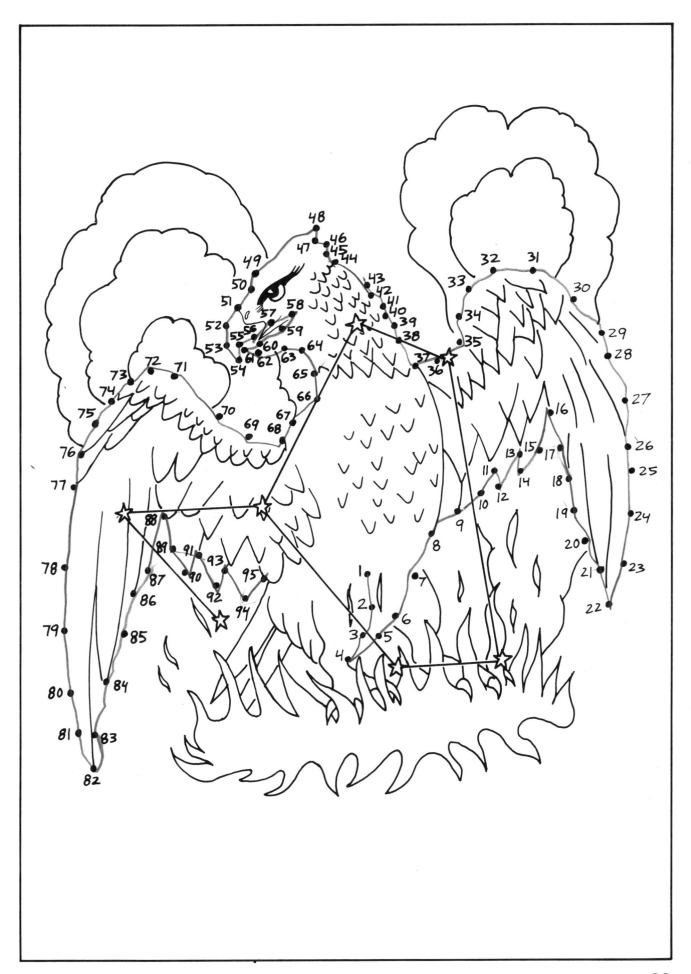

ORION, THE HUNTER

Legend: Orion was a giant and the son of Poseidon, the god of the sea. He was not afraid of any animal, and once he said that he would hunt and kill them all. This angered Gaia, the goddess of the earth. She sent a scorpion who bit and killed him—though later he was revived by Ophiuchus, the great doctor.

Number of Stars: 10, or 25 if you include arms and shield

Special Stars: One of the biggest stars, Betelgeuse is 550 to 900 times as wide across as our sun. It is at Orion's right shoulder. Rigel is one of the most luminous stars—it is as bright as 55,000 of our suns. It is located at Orion's left knee.

Star Facts: Orion's nebula, hanging from his belt, is a very big glowing cloud of gas and young stars. On a clear night, you can see it with binoculars. It looks like a tiny fuzzy patch of white light. Also in Orion is a dark cloud of gas called the Horsehead Nebula, because it looks just like the head of a horse. This constellation can be seen from both the northern and southern hemispheres.

• In ancient Egypt, they called this constellation Sirius, the God of Light, a most important god to them.

• South-Sea islanders saw it as an octopus fighting a fisherman. The line of stars across the middle (Orion's belt) was a stone ax, a weapon the fisherman used.

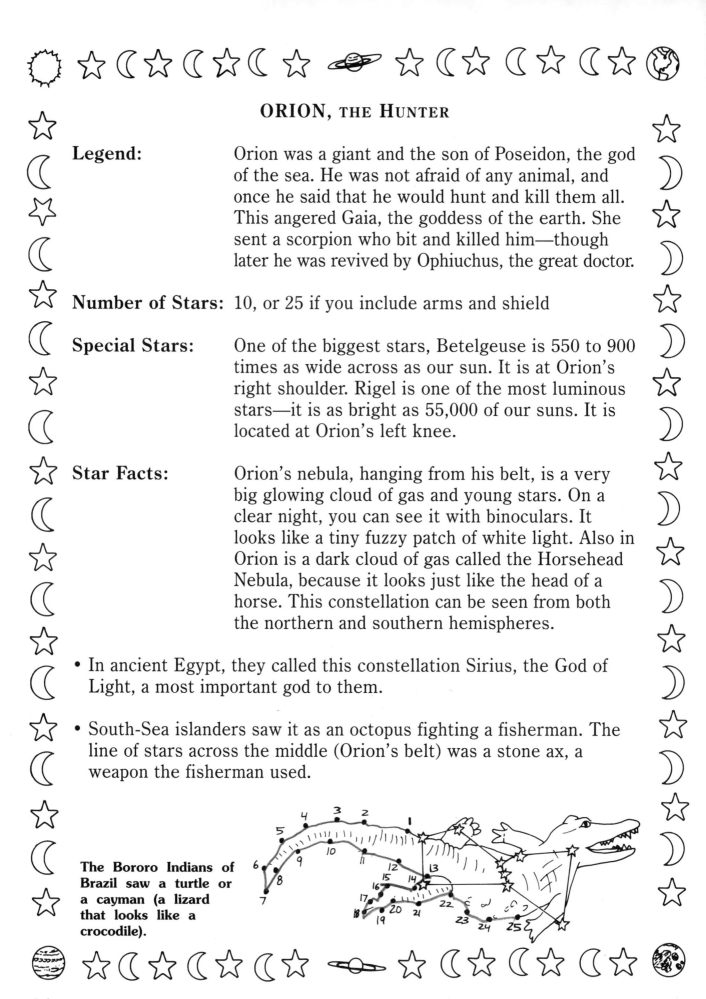

The Bororo Indians of Brazil saw a turtle or a cayman (a lizard that looks like a crocodile).

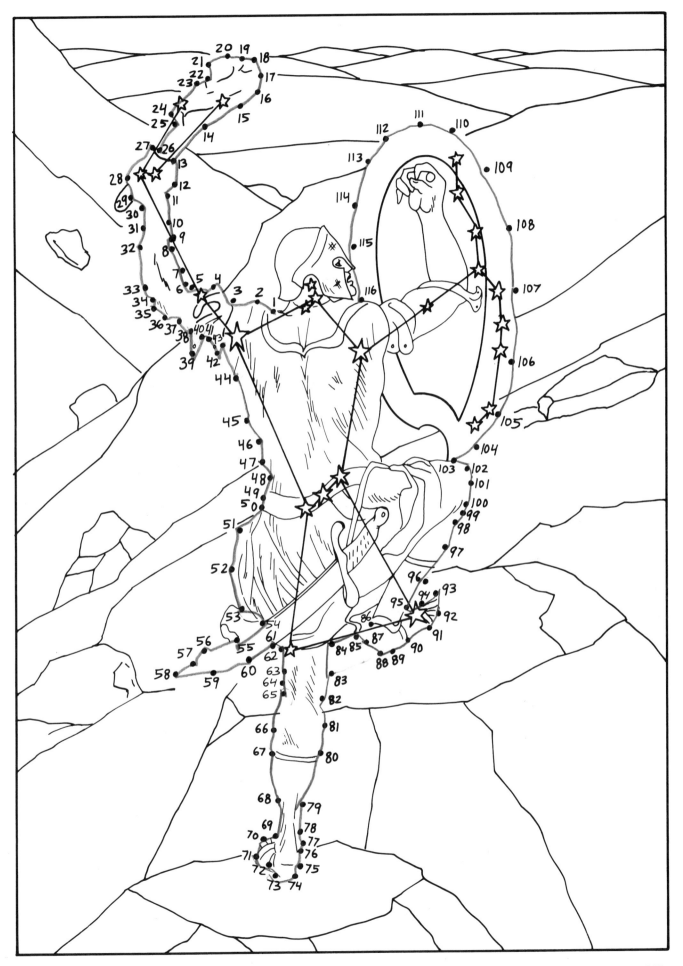

TAURUS, THE BULL

Legend: Taurus is one of the most ancient constellations. Cultures long ago thought it looked like the head of a bull with long horns. Bulls were worshipped as symbols of the earth's natural power. Taurus appears in the sky near Orion, the hunter. Sometimes in old maps of the sky Orion is shown hunting the bull.

Number of Stars: 14

Special Stars: The red star Aldebaran is the Bull's eye. A group of stars on the bull's face called the Hyades represent girls dancing in a ritual. The Pleiades is another group of stars that you can see even without binoculars. It looks like there are only six or seven of them, but with a telescope you can see about 100.

Star Facts: Taurus is one of the constellations in the zodiac. In the old Chinese zodiac it was part of the huge White Tiger.

Did You Know? Many scientists believe the universe was started by a "Big Bang"—a huge explosion—and everything in space is still moving outward from this blast that took place long ago.

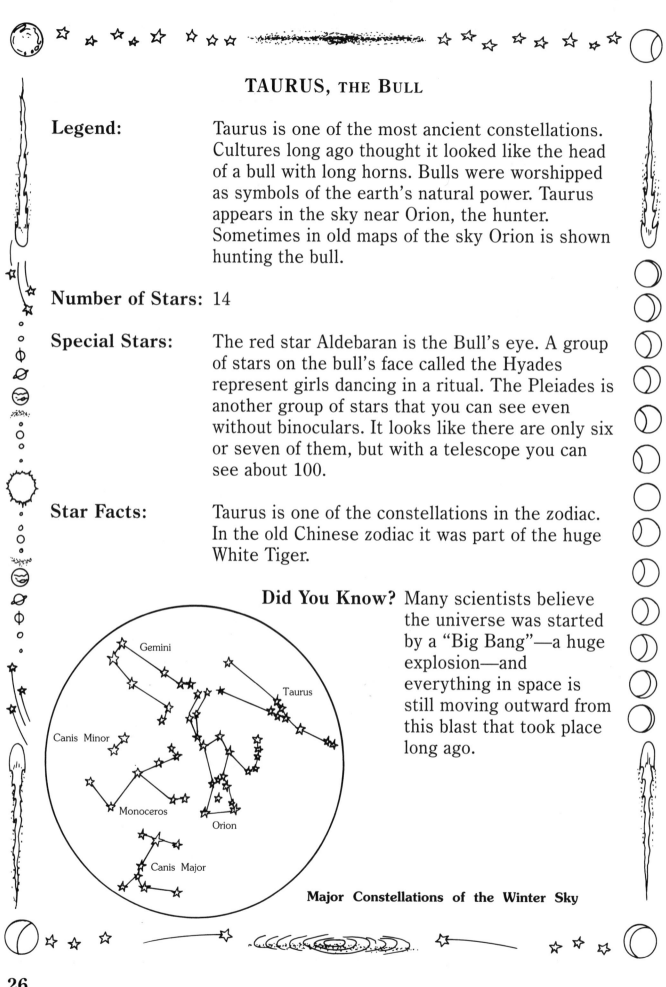

Major Constellations of the Winter Sky

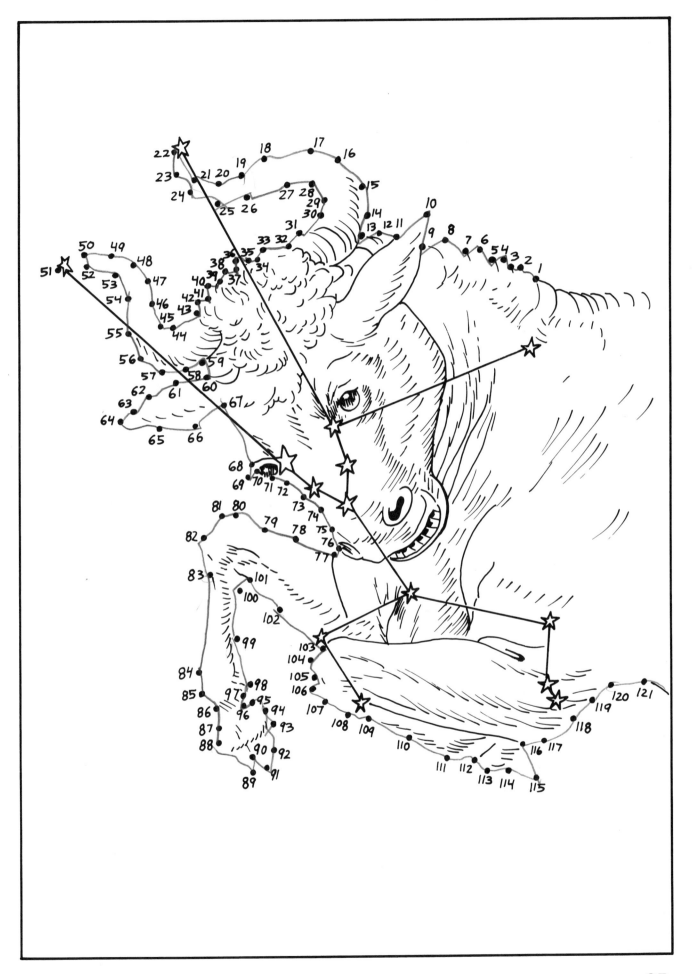

CANIS MAJOR, THE GREAT DOG

Legend: Orion had two dogs, the Great Dog and the Little Dog. They were very loyal and helped him hunt. In the sky, between the dogs is the Unicorn, a magical horse with a silver horn on its head. It is able to move so quietly that the dogs don't see it.

Number of Stars: 12

Special Stars: Sirius, is the brightest star in the whole sky—24 times as bright as our sun. It is nearer to us than most other stars, which is why it is so bright, but still so far away that it takes over 8 years for its light to travel through space to our eyes.

Star Facts: To locate Sirius, look at the stars in Orion's belt (page 24). A line connecting them points directly at Sirius.

The Chinese saw dogs, a bow and arrow, and a chicken near here. In their story, a jackal steals the chickens. Dogs chase the jackal to where the people wait with bows and arrows.

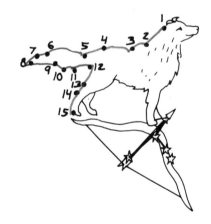

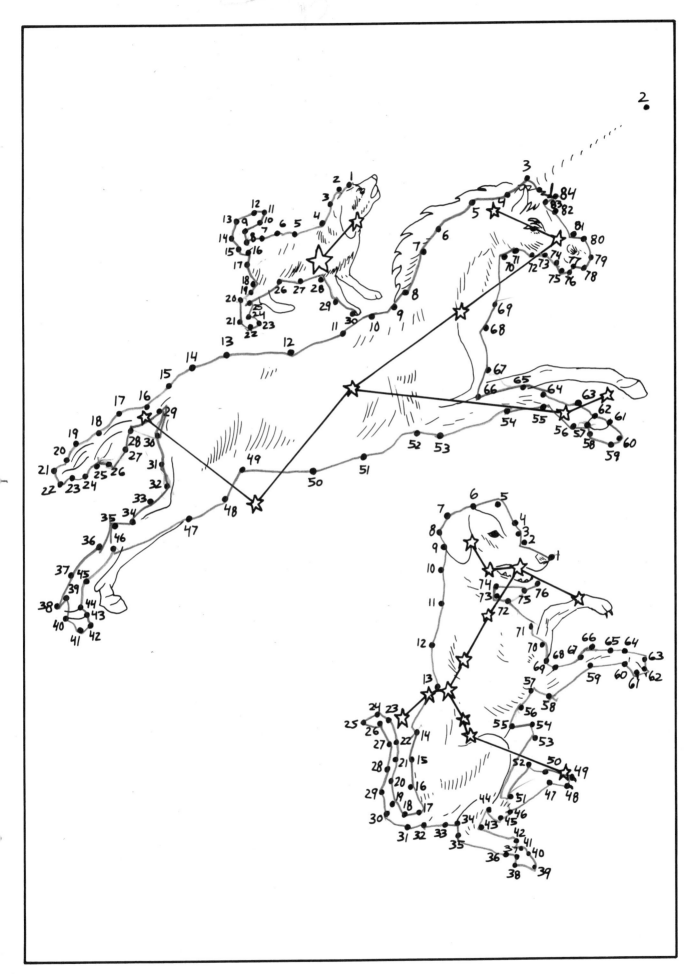

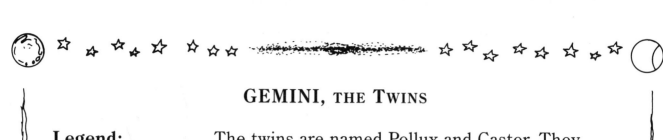

GEMINI, THE TWINS

Legend:
The twins are named Pollux and Castor. They were warrior heroes who were thought to protect sailors and help get rid of pirates and buccaneers. Pollux was immortal, but Castor was not. When Castor died, Pollux wanted to die to too, to be with his brother. But since immortals couldn't die, Jupiter allowed Pollux to spend one day with the gods and the next one in the underworld with his brother. You can see this story happening in the sky: When the stars of the twins set in the west, Castor goes first and Pollux follows.

Number of Stars: 15

Star Facts:
Gemini is one of the constellations in the zodiac.

Did You Know?
When we look up at the sky, the stars seem to be on a flat surface. Actually, the stars are all at different distances from us. It is only our view-point that makes them look flat. If we lived in a different part of the galaxy, the night sky would look very different.

• The Chinese saw many images here having to do with water. These stars helped them figure out where to dig new wells. They would look for reflections of the stars in their buckets to find the right place to dig.

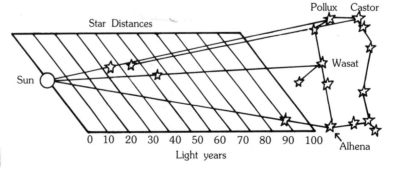

Some stars are farther away from Earth than others.

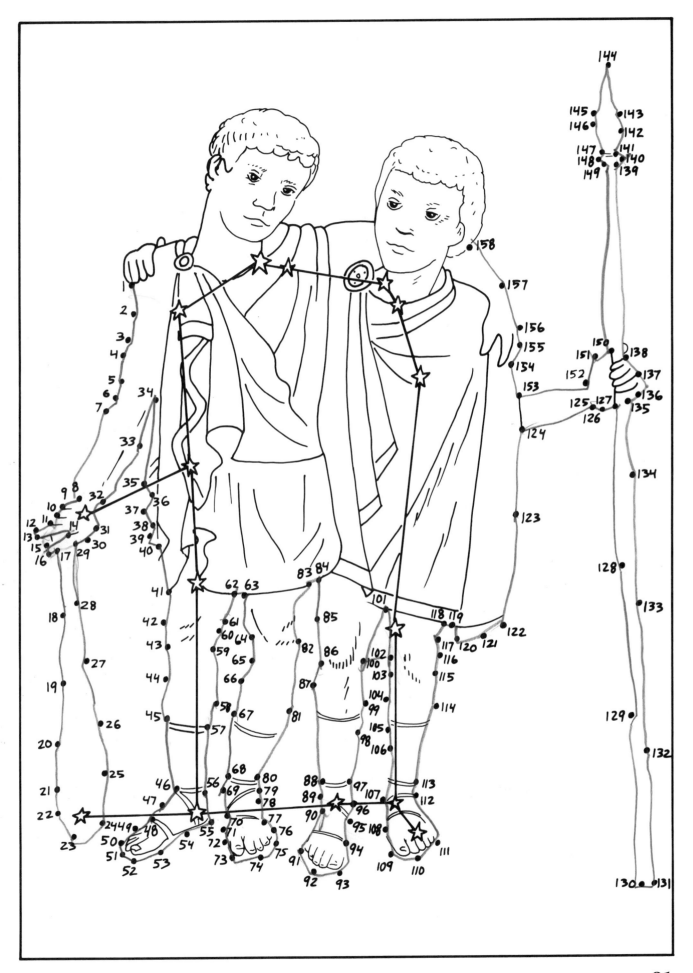

31

AURIGA, THE CHARIOTEER

Legend: In Greek myth, the gods often traveled by chariot, and charioteers like Auriga looked after the chariots of their masters as well as the animals that pulled them. Auriga holds a bridle and whip in one hand and a baby goat in the other. The goat is special to Zeus, because when he was a baby and separated from his mother, he was nursed by a goat. The brightest star in this constellation, Capella, means "little she-goat."

Number of Stars: 8

Special Stars: Capella is the sixth brightest star in the sky. Because it is so bright, and because it lies halfway between the celestial north pole and the celestial equator, sailors use it to tell which direction they are going.

Did You Know? Most stars have Arabic names. The ancient Arabs were very good astronomers, and books that they wrote about the stars were very important to astronomers of Europe. That's why we still use the names they gave the stars.

- In India, the star Capella is called the Heart of Brahma, the most important god.

- In Peru, the natives see Capella as a herder of animals.

Brahma is the Supreme Being and creator of the universe in the Hindu religion.

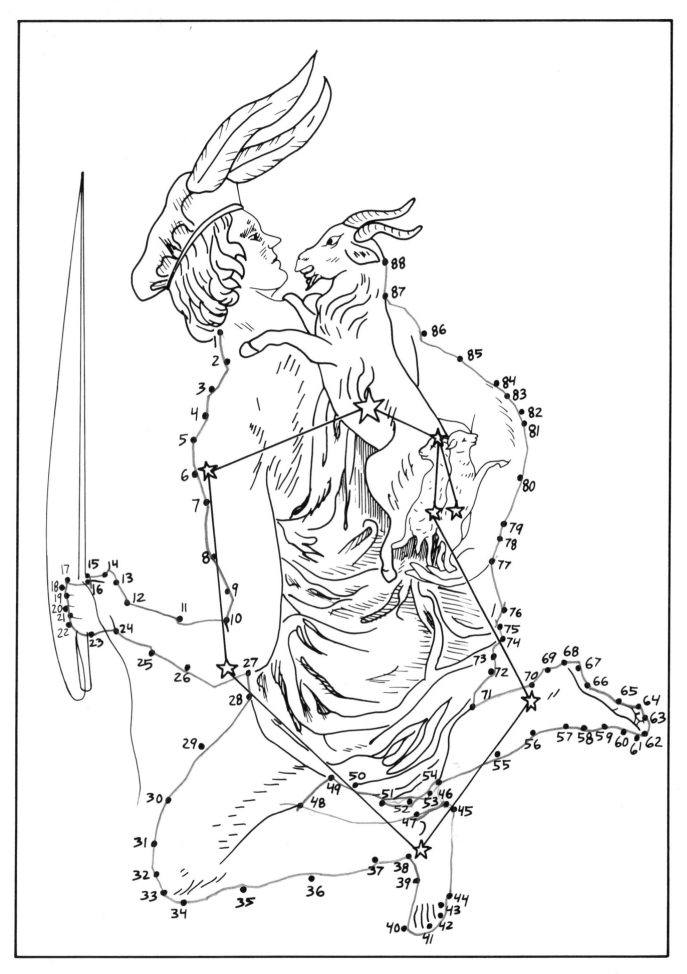

33

LEO, THE LION

Legend: One Greek story says that the Lion lived on the moon and one day came to the earth as a shooting star. He landed in the city of Corinth and caused all kinds of trouble until Hercules killed him with his bare hands. Zeus then put the Lion back in the sky where he came from.

Number of Stars: 11

Special Stars: Regulus, a blue-white star about twice as big as our sun and 120 times as bright.

Star Facts: Leo is one of the constellations in the zodiac. In the Chinese zodiac it is the Horse.

Did You Know? In the middle of November, there is a famous meteor shower in this part of the sky, called the Leonids. These showers are believed to be the remains of comets that have broken apart. Their pieces still travel the path they took a long time ago when they first traveled around the sun.

• The Taulipang Indians of northern Brazil saw a god of thunder and lightning named Tauna, and when these stars were above the horizon, it looked to them as if the figure were standing straight up. When there were heavy thunderstorms, the Indians said that Tauna was bashing the clouds.

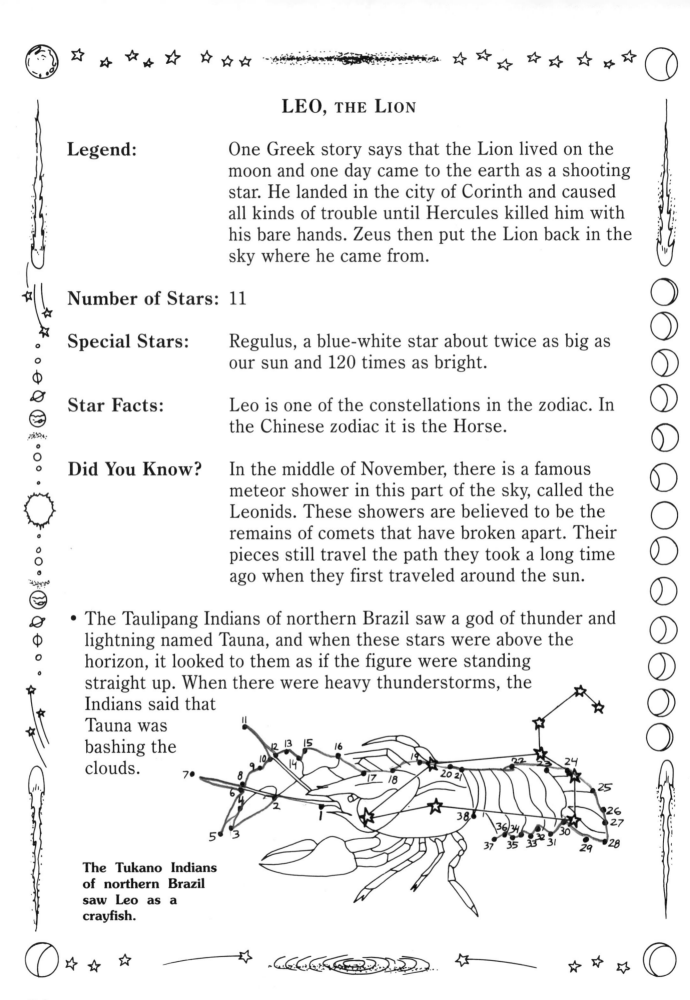

The Tukano Indians of northern Brazil saw Leo as a crayfish.

URSA MAJOR, THE GREAT BEAR

Legend: This constellation is also known as the Big Dipper, but both the Greeks and the Native Americans saw a Great Bear in these seven bright stars. In the Greek story, Zeus fell in love with the beautiful Callisto, which enraged Zeus' wife. She was so angry she turned the girl into a bear.

The Native Americans have a story that after midnight, forest trees move around and visit each other. One night, a bear lost his way, and when the trees started moving, he kept crashing into them by accident. This angered one of the oak trees, who chased the bear but couldn't catch him. The chase went on until sunrise, when the tree finally caught the bear by the tail and tossed him into the sky.

Number of Stars: 7 or 20, depending on whether you're looking at the Big Dipper or the Great Bear. The bear has more stars in it.

Special Stars: Mizar and Alcor are the best known double stars (two stars so close together that they look like one star). You can see both without binoculars.

Star Facts: Five of the stars in this constellation are quite close to each other. They are all moving together through space very fast—525 miles per minute. That's almost a million miles a day.

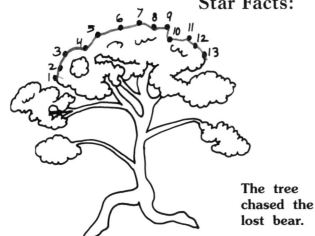

The tree chased the lost bear.

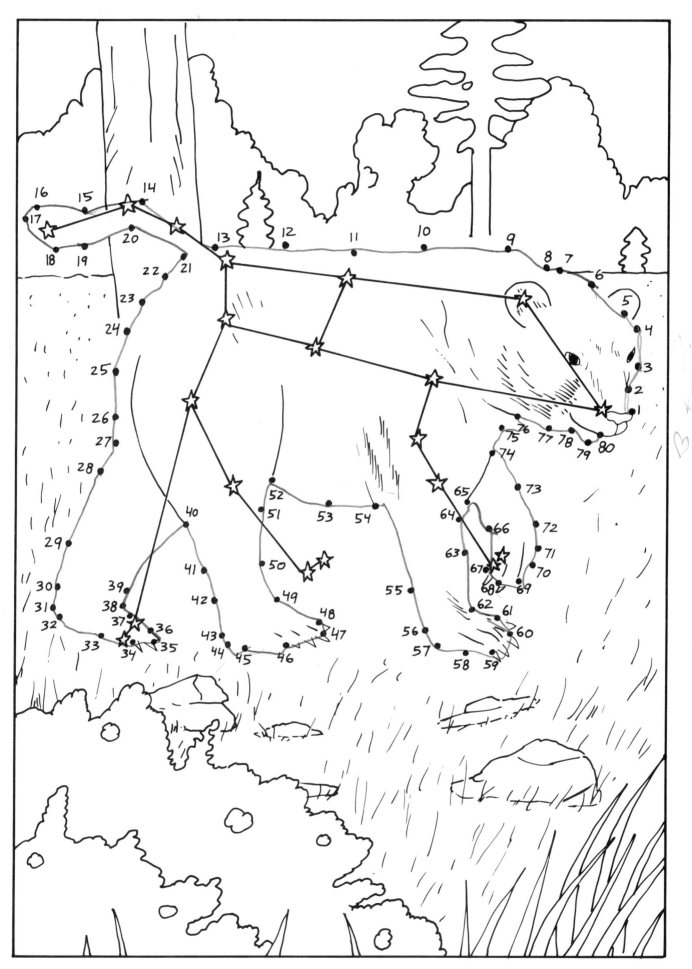

URSA MINOR, THE LITTLE BEAR

Legend: Ursa Minor is also known as the Little Dipper. In the Greek legend, before Callisto was turned into a bear, she and Zeus had a son named Arcas. Once, as Arcas walked through the woods, his mother, in the shape of a bear, ran toward him to hug him. He was about to shoot her with his bow and arrow when Zeus turned him into a little bear, and put them both in the sky. Together, Callisto and Arcas make the Great Bear and the Little Bear. The story goes that the bears both got their really long tails when Zeus pulled them up into the heavens.

Number of Stars: 8 (One is a double star, so it looks like only 7.)

Special Stars: One of the best known stars, Polaris, the North Star, is in this constellation, pointing to the north.

- The Egyptians saw a hippopotamus in these stars, which stood for the heavens and the cosmic mother or Mother Nature.

Since the northern stars never set, sometimes they were considered evil. So the Egyptians said the hippopotamus kept these mean stars from doing any harm.

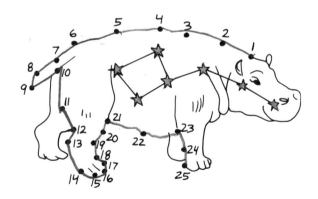

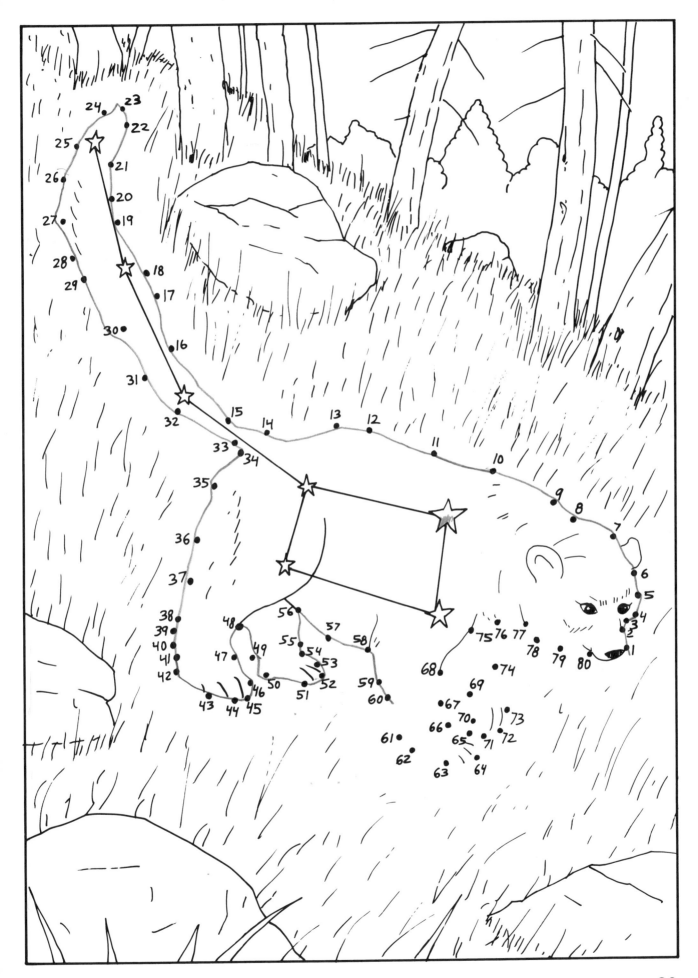

CANCER, THE CRAB

Legend: Hera, queen of the gods in Greek mythology, always hated Hercules because he was the son of Zeus and a mortal woman. She tried to kill him many times. When Hercules was given the job of killing the Hydra, a nine-headed water serpent, she sent a crab to stop him. The crab bit Hercules' foot and he crushed its shell, killing the crab and then the Hydra. Hera set the image of the crab in the sky as a reward for its services.

Number of Stars: 5

Special Stars: Very few bright stars are in the Crab.

Star Facts: Cancer is one of the constellations in the zodiac.

• The Egyptians saw their sacred beetle, the Scarab, in the stars of Cancer.

To the Egyptians, scarabs were symbols of birth and everlasting life.

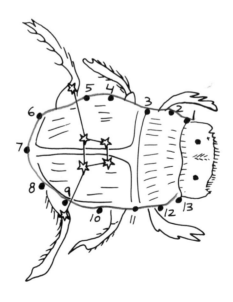

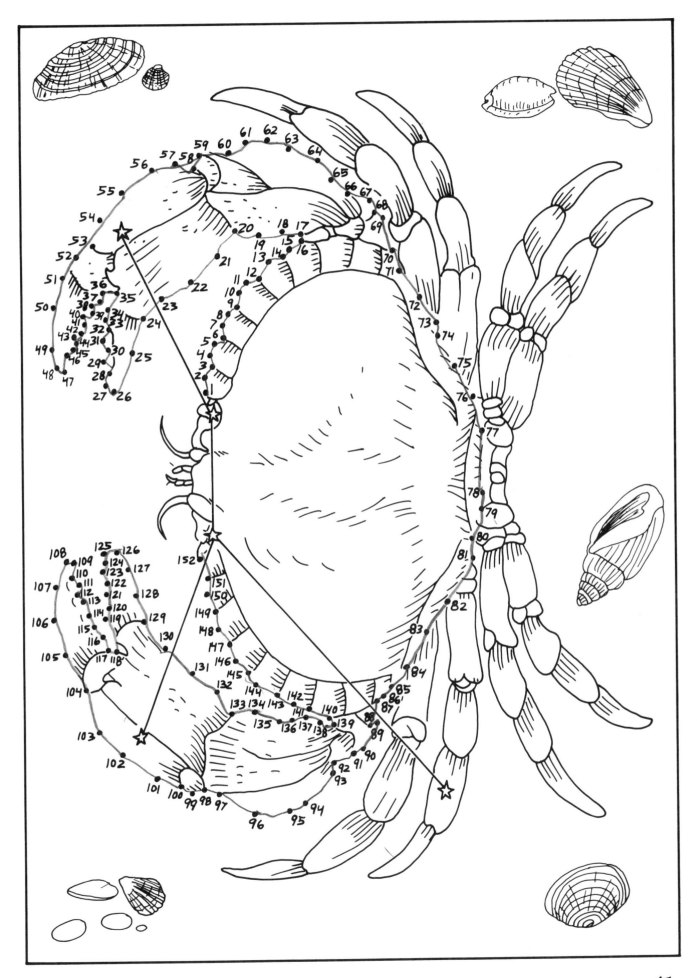

41

BOOTES, THE HERDSMAN, AND
CANES VENATICI, THE HUNTING DOGS

Legend: Bootes is seen as a bear driver who chases the Great Bear and the Little Bear around the Pole Star—or perhaps protects them. In another story, Bootes was a grape grower who was friendly to Bacchus, the god of Wine, when he was in disguise. Bacchus taught Bootes to make wine from grapes. Bootes invited many people to a party to drink the wine he made. Everyone got sick, blamed Bootes, and killed him. His dogs missed him and went to die with their master.

Number of Stars: 14

Special Stars: Arcturus is a giant orange-colored star, 27 times the size of our sun. It is one of the brightest and hottest stars in our sky. The three stars in the tail of the Great Bear (the Big Dipper) point to Arcturus.

The Kobeua Indians of northern Brazil saw Bootes as a man-eating fish called a piranha.

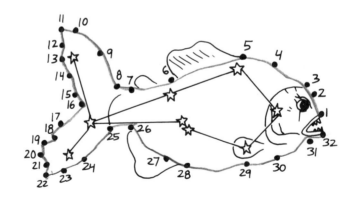

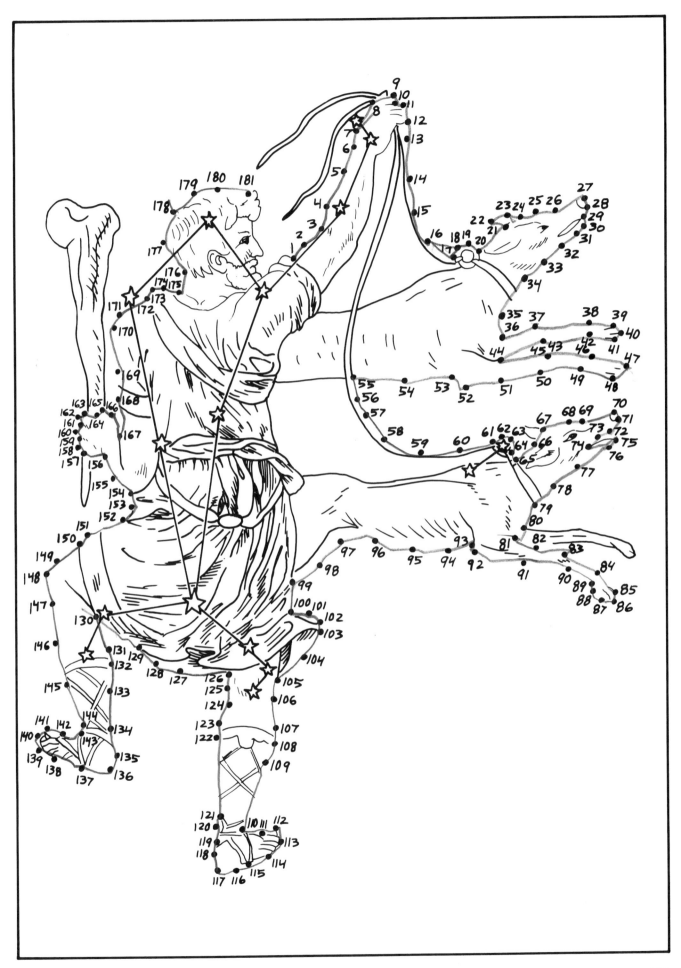

VIRGO, THE MAIDEN

Legend: The Greeks thought of Virgo as Demeter, the goddess of the fields, and also as her beautiful daughter Persephone. Persephone was kidnapped by Hades, god of the underworld, who had fallen in love with her. Demeter was so sad over the loss of her daughter that all the crops died. Zeus decided that Persephone could come back to her mother for half the year, but she had to spend the other half in the underworld with Hades. This is how the seasons were created. When mother and daughter are together, it is spring and summer and everything grows. When they are apart, it is fall and winter, and the fields lie empty.

Number of Stars: 14

Special Stars: Spica, at the maiden's left hand, is a very bright, hot star—as bright as 1,600 suns. *Spica* is Latin for "ear of wheat."

There is a group of about 3,000 galaxies in this region of the sky. It is called the Virgo cluster. You need a telescope to see most of them.

Star Facts: Virgo, second largest of all the constellations, is one of the constellations in the zodiac. It is the only female figure among the 12 constellations of the zodiac.

Major Constellations of the Spring Sky

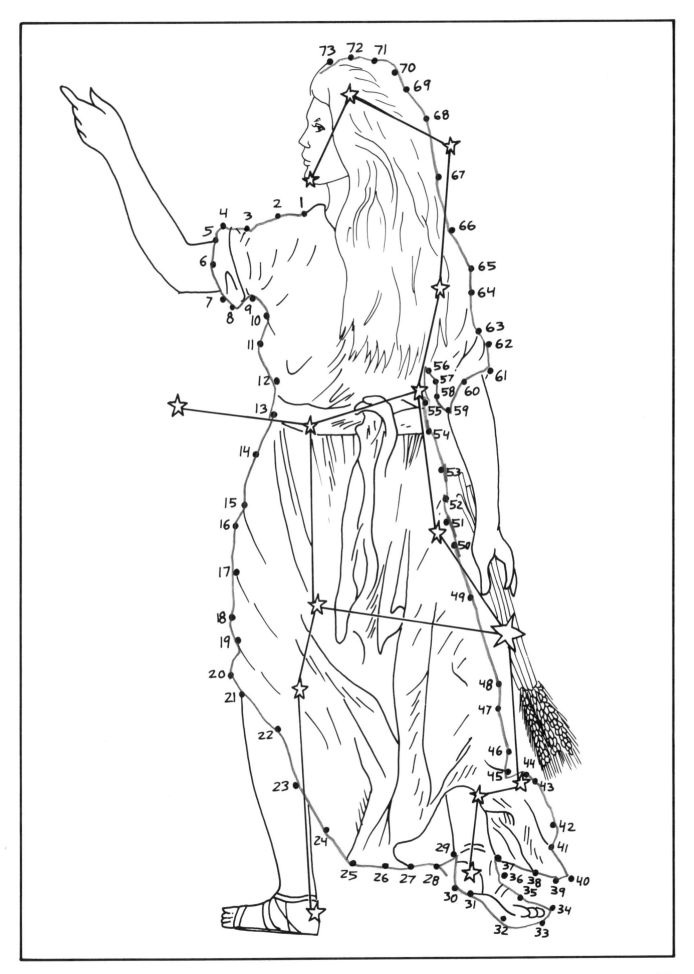

HYDRA, THE SEA-SERPENT, AND CORVUS, THE CROW

Legend: The Hydra was a vicious nine-headed sea-serpent with a doglike body. Its breath—even its smell—was fatal, but it could not be killed because one of its heads was immortal. Hercules finally did manage to kill it by setting fire to it, cutting off the immortal head, and burying it. But it was because of Corvus, the crow, that the Hydra ended up as a constellation. Corvus was supposed to fetch a cup of water for Apollo, god of the sun. Corvus stopped to eat some figs, and when he was late getting back, he blamed it on Hydra. Apollo knew this was a lie. So he put the crow, the cup of water, and Hydra all up in the sky, and made the crow ride on Hydra's back. The crow got very thirsty, but couldn't reach the cup of water, because Hydra's back was so long.

Number of Stars: 23

Star Facts: Hydra is the largest and longest constellation.

Did You Know? Planets are different from stars. Stars are all burning balls of gas that make their own light. Planets are made of rock and water and gas, like Earth, or of gas, like Jupiter. Planets orbit stars—the way Earth revolves around the sun. Venus looks like a star in our sky, but it doesn't make its own light. It just reflects sunlight very brightly.

Sun or Star

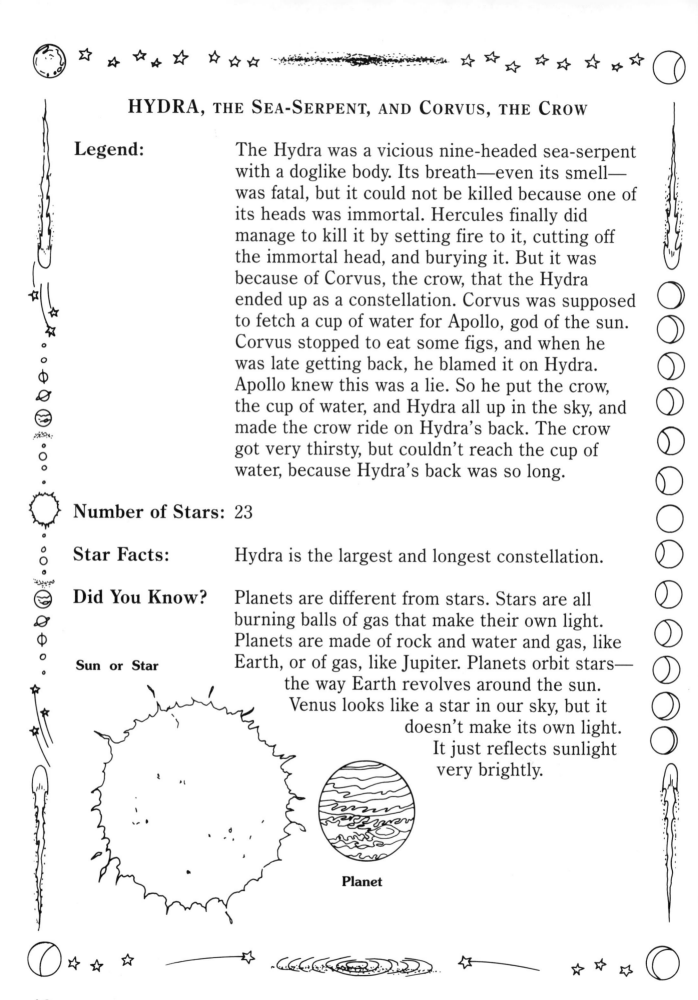

Planet

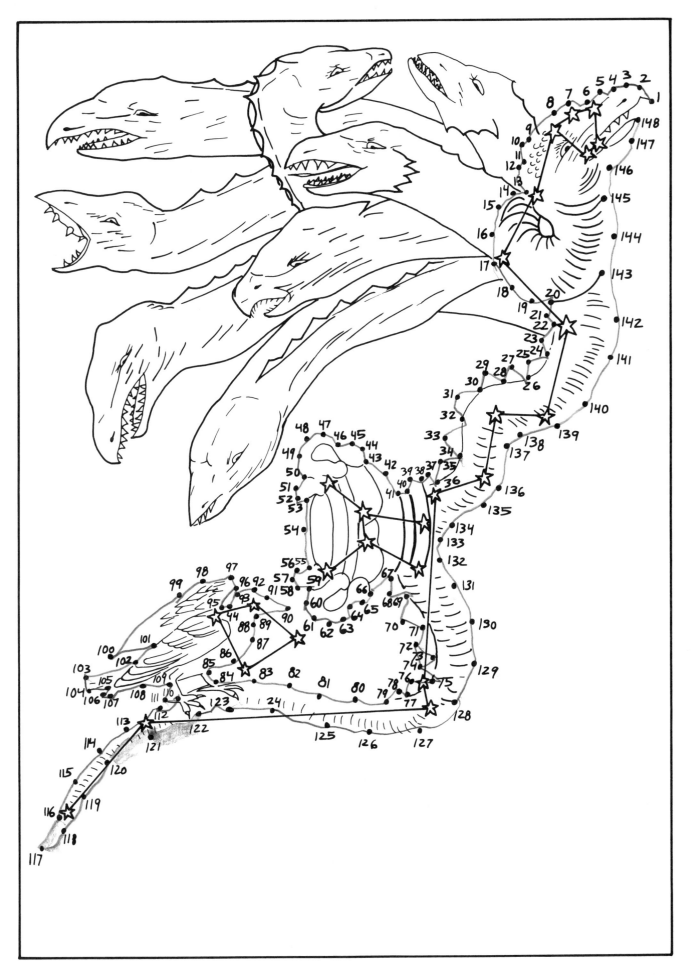

CYGNUS, THE SWAN

Legend: A Greek legend tells about Phaethon, Apollo's son, who insisted that his father let him drive the sun chariot for a day. Apollo didn't have time to instruct his son properly, and when the horses felt an unfamiliar hand on the reins, they flew too high and too low, causing great damage to the earth. Zeus sent a thunderbolt, and Phaethon fell to the earth like a shooting star, landing in the river. Phaethon's best friend, Cygnus, did all he could to gather together his friend's bones, diving again and again into the waters of the river. Zeus was so impressed at Cygnus' devotion to his friend that he turned him into a beautiful swan and placed him among the stars, right in the path of the Milky Way.

Number of Stars: 10

Special Stars: Deneb is a bright star that marks the tail of the swan. It is one of the biggest and brightest supergiants, as wide as 60 of our suns, and as bright as 60,000 of them.

Star Facts: This constellation is also called the Northern Cross.

Did You Know? Near the tail of the Swan, in the Milky Way, is a bright cloud of hydrogen gas, shaped like the continent of North America.

• In China this constellation was sometimes called one of the magpies that formed a bridge across the River of Heaven (see pages 52–53).

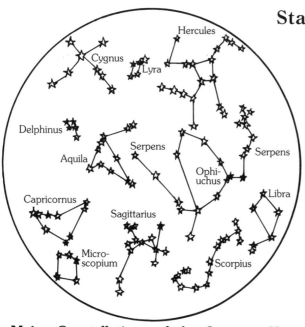

Major Constellations of the Summer Sky

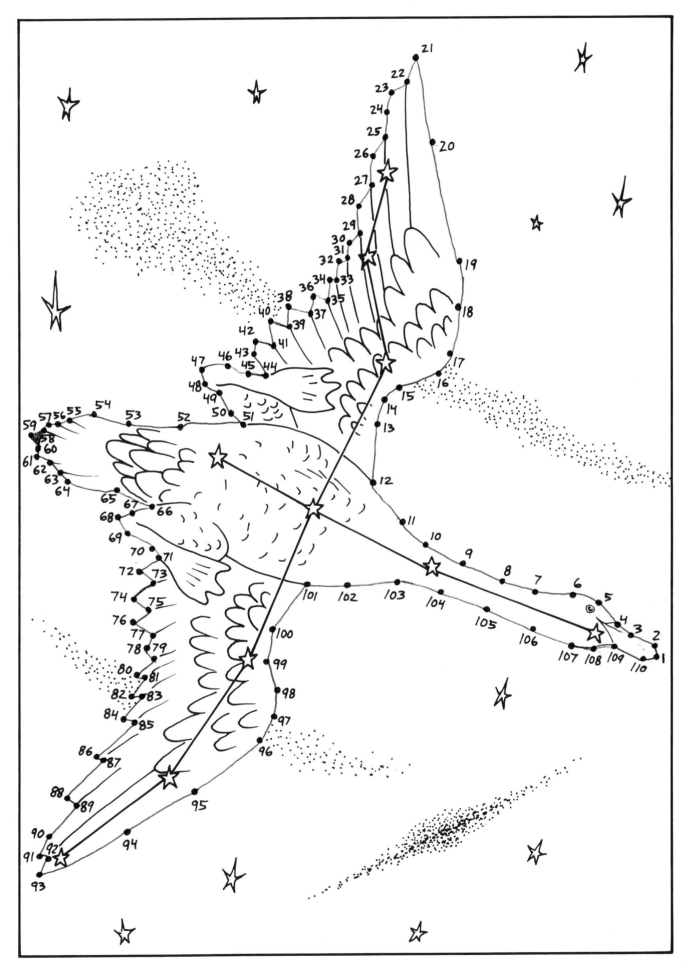

AQUILA, THE EAGLE

Legend: Aquila was Zeus's bird, who performed many tasks for him. It was Aquila who had to punish Prometheus for stealing fire. Zeus had Prometheus chained and sent Aquila to eat his liver every day. Every day Prometheus's liver would grow back, and Aquila would eat it again. At last, one day, Hercules set Prometheus free by killing the Eagle with a poisoned arrow. Then Zeus put Aquila among the stars in thanks for his good work.

Number of Stars: 8

Special Stars: Altair, a brilliant star, is one of the nearest stars to us.

Did You Know? Stars don't live forever. They are born where lots of gas and dust gather together. After billions of years, their gas burns up. As the stars get old, they puff up and change color. These old stars are called red giants. Some stars end with a big explosion. Others burn out quietly and fade away.

• Many cultures have seen this constellation as an eagle. The Arabs called it Black Eagle. The Turks called it Hunting Eagle. The Hebrews called it Eagle, Falcon, or Vulture.

The Life Cycle of a Star

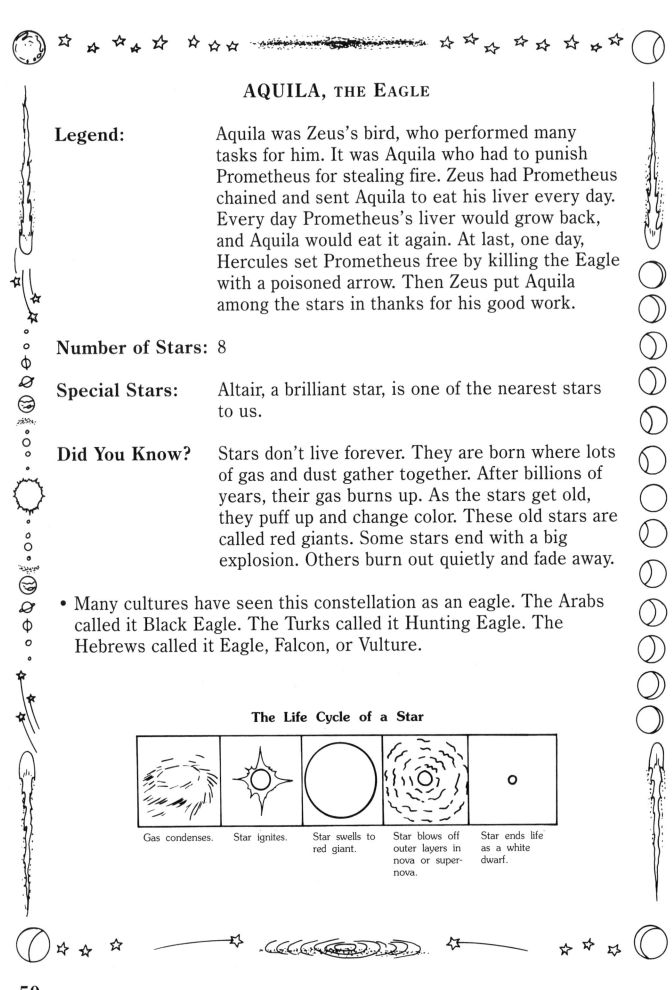

| Gas condenses. | Star ignites. | Star swells to red giant. | Star blows off outer layers in nova or super-nova. | Star ends life as a white dwarf. |

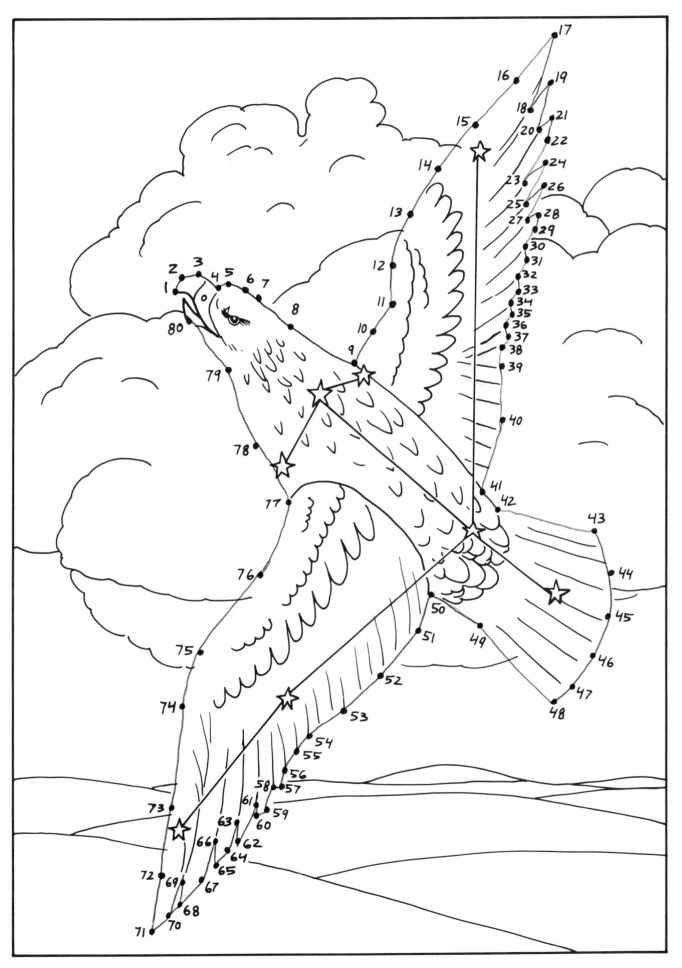

51

LYRA, THE HARP

Legend: Hermes, the messenger of the gods, invented the harp. He traded it to Apollo, god of the sun, who gave it to his son Orpheus. Orpheus learned to play the harp so well that he could charm wild beasts.

In a story from China, the Weaving Princess fell in love with a cowherd. They were so happy together that they neglected their chores. So the king separated them across the River of Heaven. They were allowed to meet once a year on a bridge made of birds. In the sky, Vega, who represents the princess, lies on one side of the Milky Way, and the bright star, Altair, the cowherd, lies on the other side in the constellation Aquila.

Number of Stars: 5

Special Stars: The brightest star in Lyra is called Vega. In Asia, Vega represents the Weaving Princess.

Did You Know? The Ring Nebula, in Lyra, is a beautiful cloud of gas that looks like a smoke ring when you see it through a telescope. It was created when a star exploded.

• Ancient cultures of the Middle East and India saw Vega as a vulture.

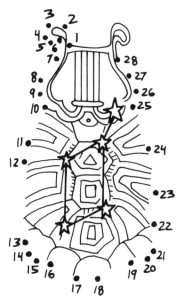

Hermes invented the harp by putting strings on an empty tortoise shell.

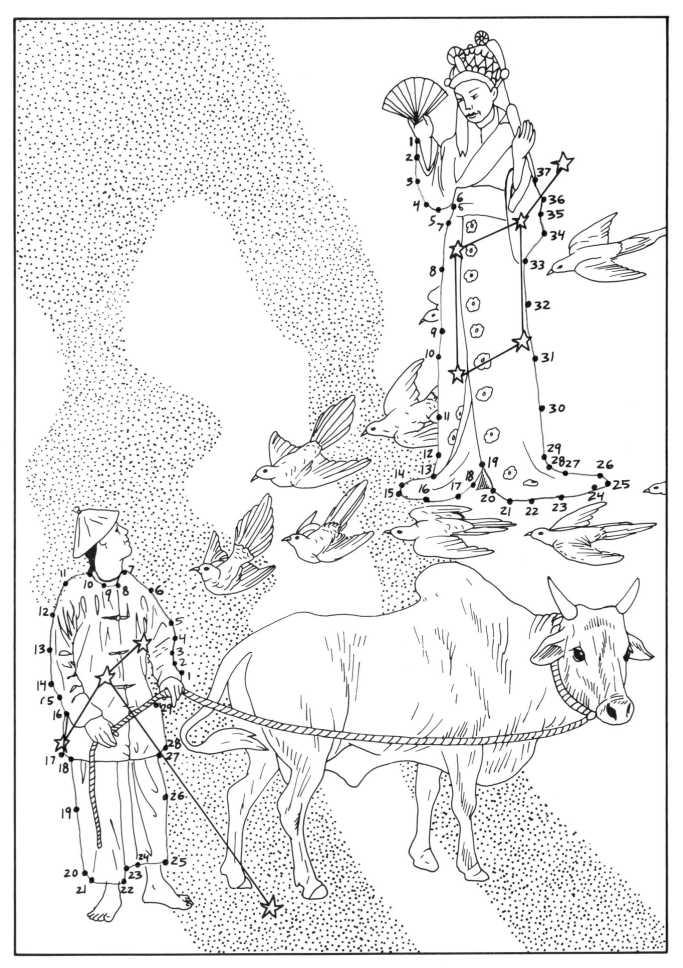

53

HERCULES, THE STRONG MAN

Legend:
In Greek myth, Hercules was the son of Zeus, king of the gods, and a mortal woman. Even as a little baby, he was fantastically strong. Hercules became famous for doing 12 almost impossible tasks, such as capturing a wild boar, fighting Cerberus, the hell hound, an enormous lion, and man-eating birds, and fetching fruit from the golden apple tree guarded by an ever-watchful dragon. In the end, Zeus raised Hercules among the gods and placed him in the sky.

Number of Stars: 23

Special Stars:
The star Alpha Hercules (its Latin and Greek name) or Ras Algethi (its Arabic name) is one of the biggest known stars. This huge star is called a red supergiant. It is about 500 times larger than our sun, and 10,000 times brighter.

Cerberus was the three-headed dog that guarded the underworld.

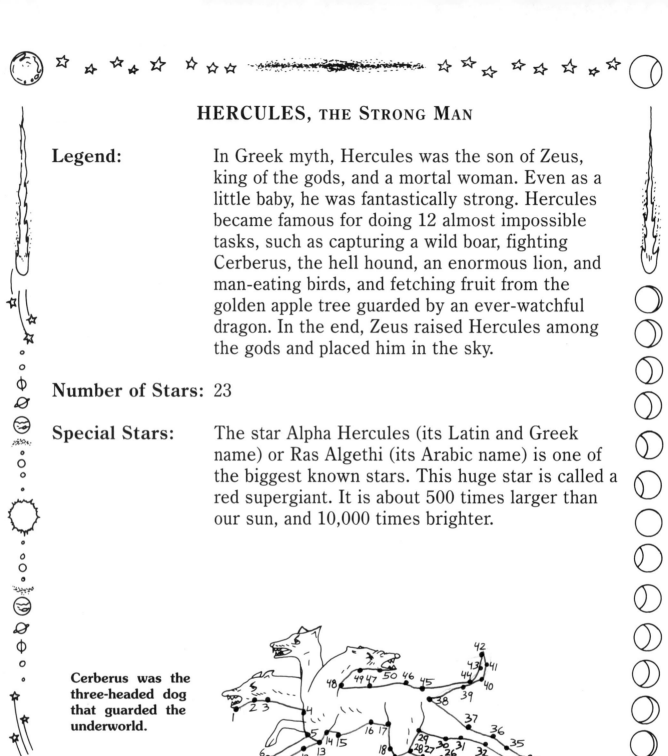

DELPHINUS, THE DOLPHIN

Legend: Poseidon, god of the sea, once fell in love with a mermaid. The Dolphin, a friend of men and gods, carried Poseidon on his back to help him pursue the mermaid. The playful Dolphin also followed the mermaid wherever she went and told her nice things about Poseidon. Finally, she agreed to marry him. Another story tells of the Greek poet Arion who was attacked by pirates at sea. He sang a song calling the dolphins to him. When the pirates threw him overboard, a dolphin carried him to shore.

Number of Stars: 6

Special Stars: Two stars in Delphinus have very unusual names—Sualocin and Rotanev. No one knew what these names meant for a long time. Finally, someone noticed that these names were the name of an astronomer, Nicolaus Venator, spelled backwards.

Did You Know? Only two people from recent times have their names in the stars. The astronomer Nicolaus Venator is one. The other is King Charles II of England. His star, Cor Caroli, or "The Heart of Charles" is in the constellation of Canes Venatici (the hunting dogs).

The Dolphin helped to match up a mermaid with the god of the sea.

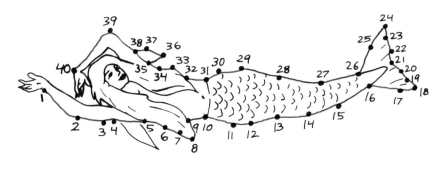

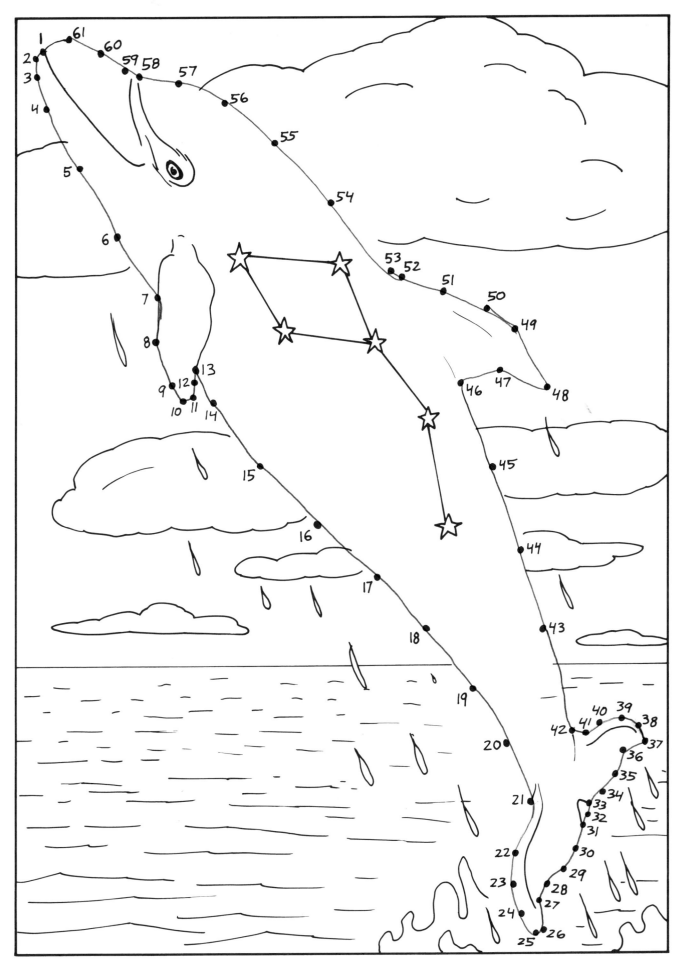

OPHIUCHUS, THE SERPENT-BEARER

Legend: Ophiuchus was a famous doctor. He was taught medicine by Chiron, a centaur (half man, half horse). He learned the secret of healing herbs from snakes. He could even bring people back from the dead. Hades, god of the dead, didn't want anyone to have this power, so he had Zeus strike Ophiuchus down with a lightning bolt. Some stories say that Aquila, the Eagle, delivered the lightning bolt. You can see Aquila flying just above Ophiuchus in the night sky. Another name for Ophiuchus is Aesculapius.

Number of Stars: 15

Special Stars: In 1604, a supernova—an exploding star— appeared in this constellation. It was visible for two years before it faded away.

Did You Know? The modern symbol for doctors and medicine is a staff with two snakes wrapped around it. This symbol comes from the story of the two snakes who taught Ophiuchus about herbs.

• In ancient Babylon, this constellation was called Marduk, the Sea God, who fought with the sea-serpent Tiamat.

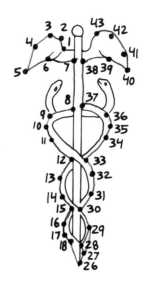

This symbol of doctors is called a "Cadeuces" (pronounced "K'DOO-shus").

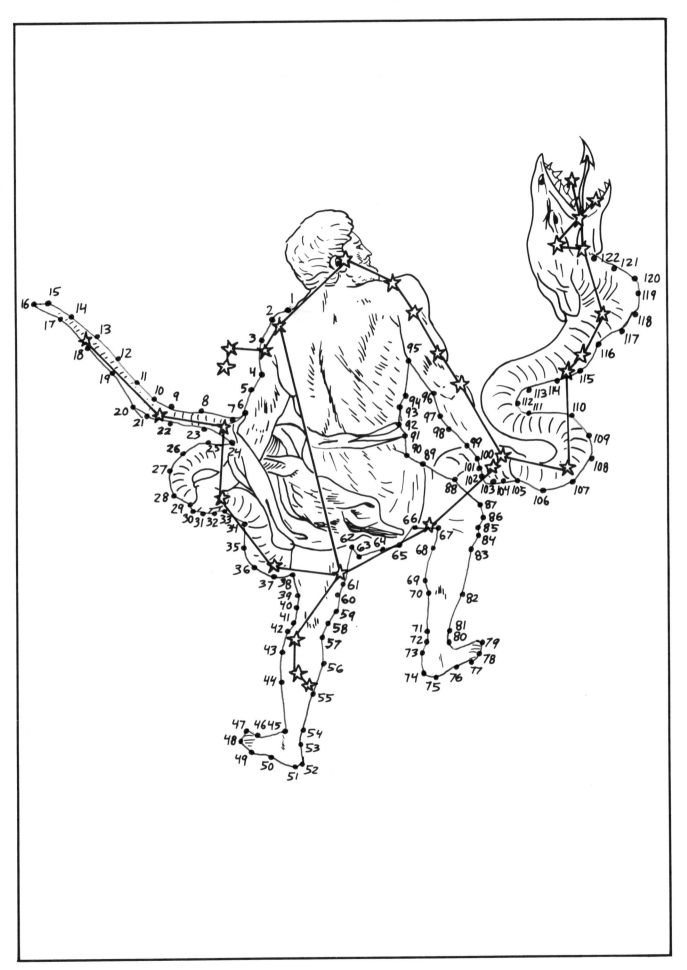

LIBRA, THE SCALES

Legend:　In Roman times when the sun entered Libra it was the first day of fall, when the length of day and night are the same. This is part of what the Scales show. Scales weigh two things, balancing one against the other, meaning that there is fairness and peace.

Number of Stars: 8

Star Facts:　Libra is one of the constellations in the zodiac. In Chinese astrology it was originally the sign of the Dragon. Later it became the sign of long life.

Did You Know?　Stars are so far away that it takes years for their light to reach us. When we look at the stars in the sky, we are seeing the way they looked many years ago, as that light finally arrives where we are today. It's like looking back in time.

Sometimes a hermit bird is seen just below the Scales.

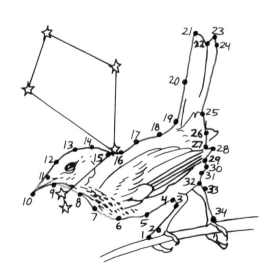

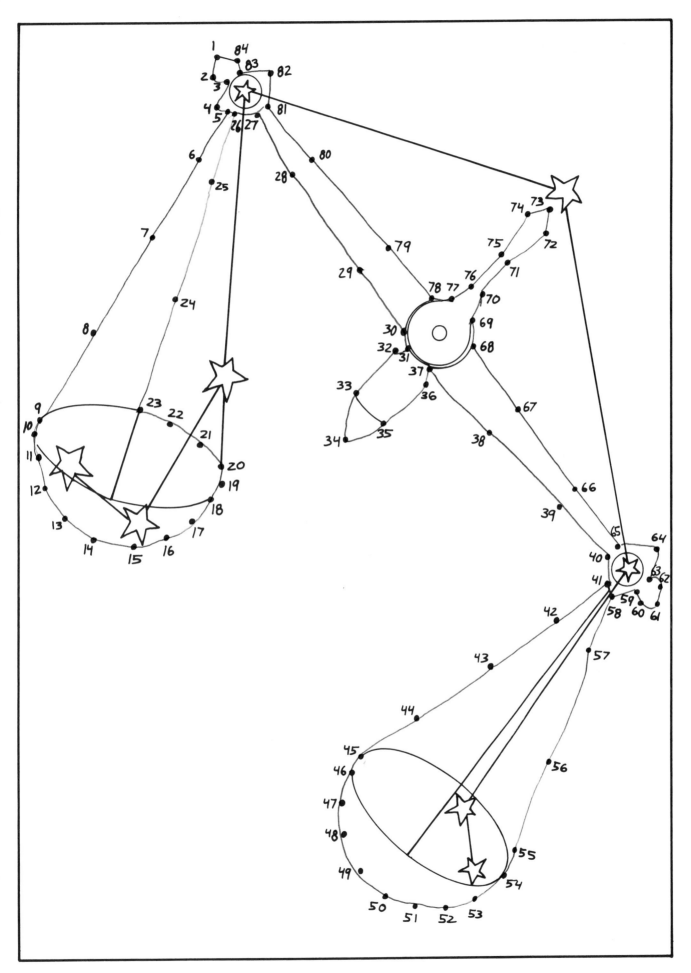

61

SCORPIUS, THE SCORPION

Legend: When Orion, the hunter, said he would kill all the animals on the earth, Gaia, the goddess of the earth, sent Scorpius to sting him. The Scorpion bit him on the heel and killed him. You can see this story played out in the sky. When Orion sets in the sky at night, the constellation of the Scorpion is just rising in the east.

Number of Stars: 20 (Two are double stars.)

Special Stars: Antares is a red supergiant at the heart of the scorpion. It is very large—300 times the size of the sun. If the sun were that big, we'd be inside it! Even Mars would be inside it! Because of Antares' position in the sky, the moon often passes right in front of it, blocking out its light for an hour or two.

Star Facts: Scorpio is one of the constellations of the zodiac.

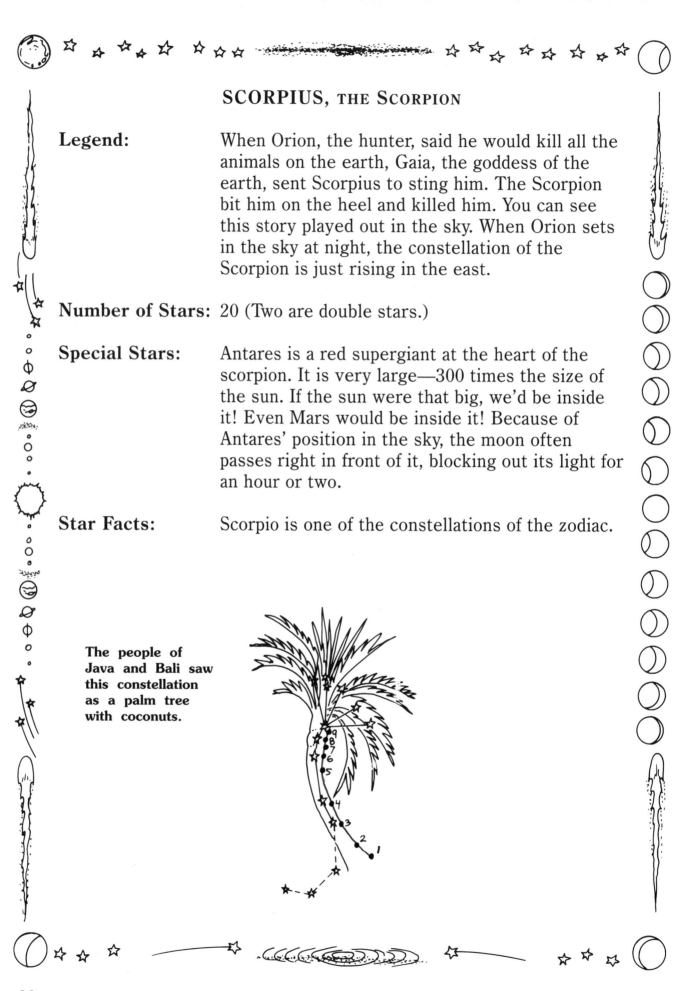

The people of Java and Bali saw this constellation as a palm tree with coconuts.

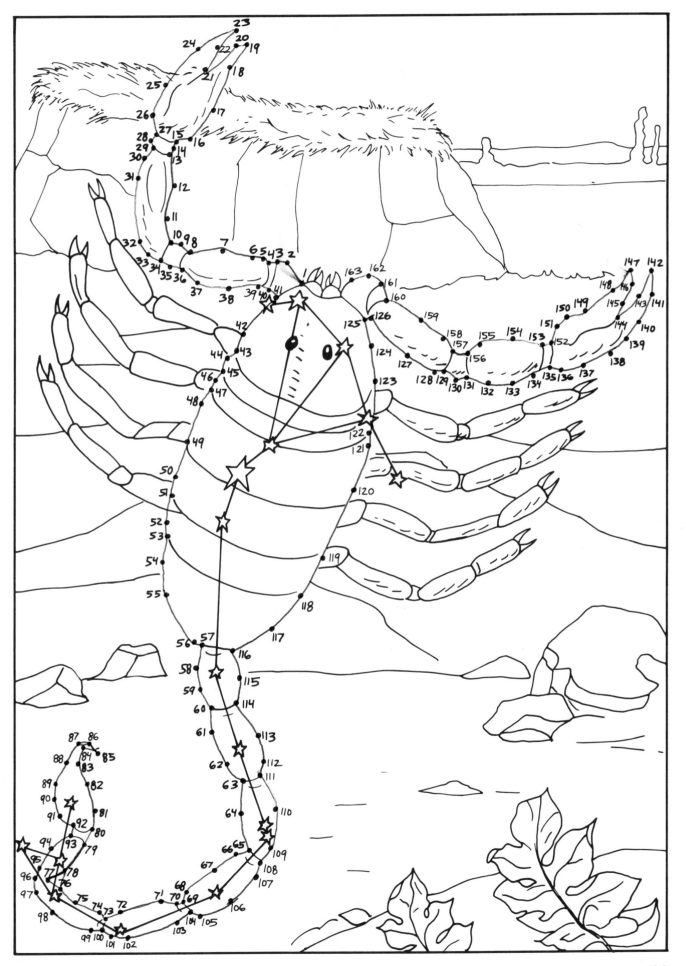

SAGITTARIUS, THE ARCHER

Legend: Sagittarius was a centaur—half man, half horse. He hunted Scorpius, the Scorpion, with a bow and arrow because Scorpius stung his friend Orion, the Hunter.

Number of Stars: 24

Star Facts: Sagittarius is one of the constellations of the zodiac.

Did You Know?   When you look at Sagittarius in the sky, you are looking toward the center of our galaxy.

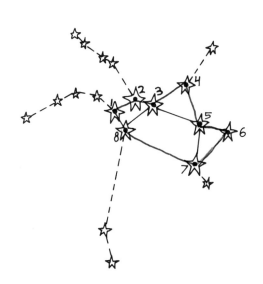

The eight brightest stars of Sagittarius look like a teapot.

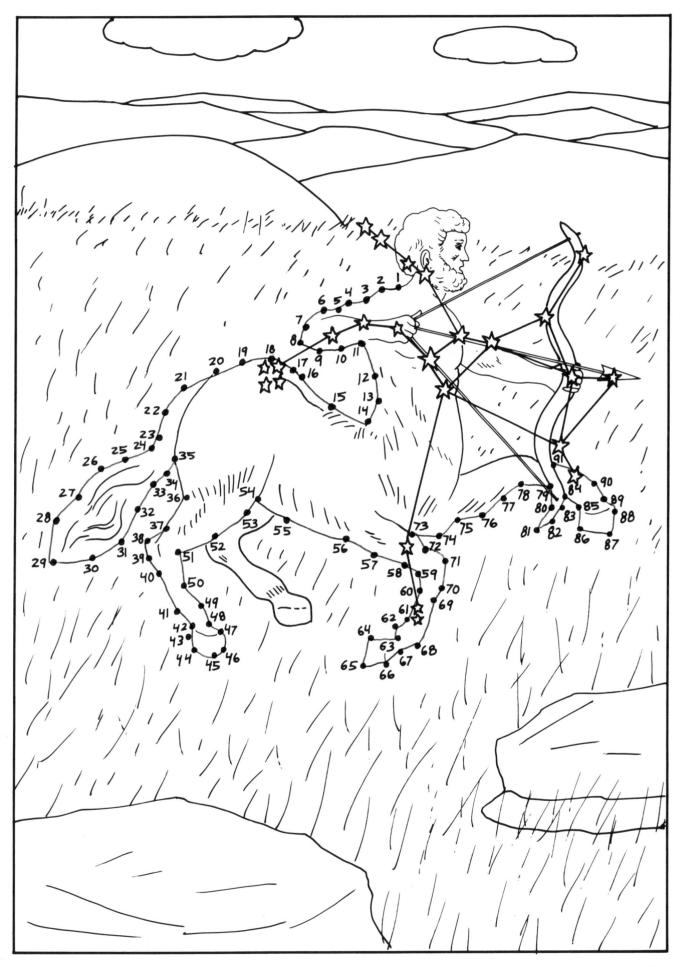

CAPRICORNUS, THE SEA-GOAT

Legend:
Pan, the god of nature, in the form of a goat, was playing his pipes by a river. A monster named Typhon began chasing him, and without thinking, Pan turned himself into a fish so he could swim away in the water. But the whole thing happened so quickly that only his rear end was transformed. It became a fish's tail, and that's how Pan became half goat and half fish. Later, when Zeus was fighting Typhon and needed help, Pan blew his horn very loudly, bringing other gods to the rescue. Zeus thanked Pan by creating the constellation of Capricornus.

Number of Stars: 13

Star Facts:
Capricornus is one of the constellations of the zodiac. Looking south from anywhere north of the equator—at the end of July or the beginning of August—you can see Capricornus at midnight.

• The Egyptians saw this constellation as a fish or a mirror.

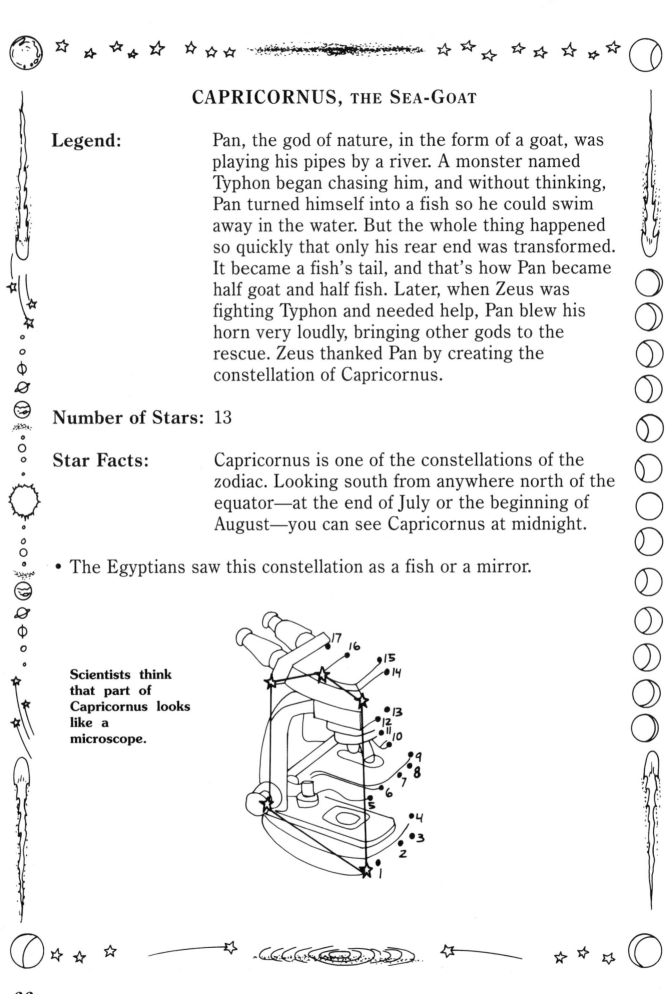

Scientists think that part of Capricornus looks like a microscope.

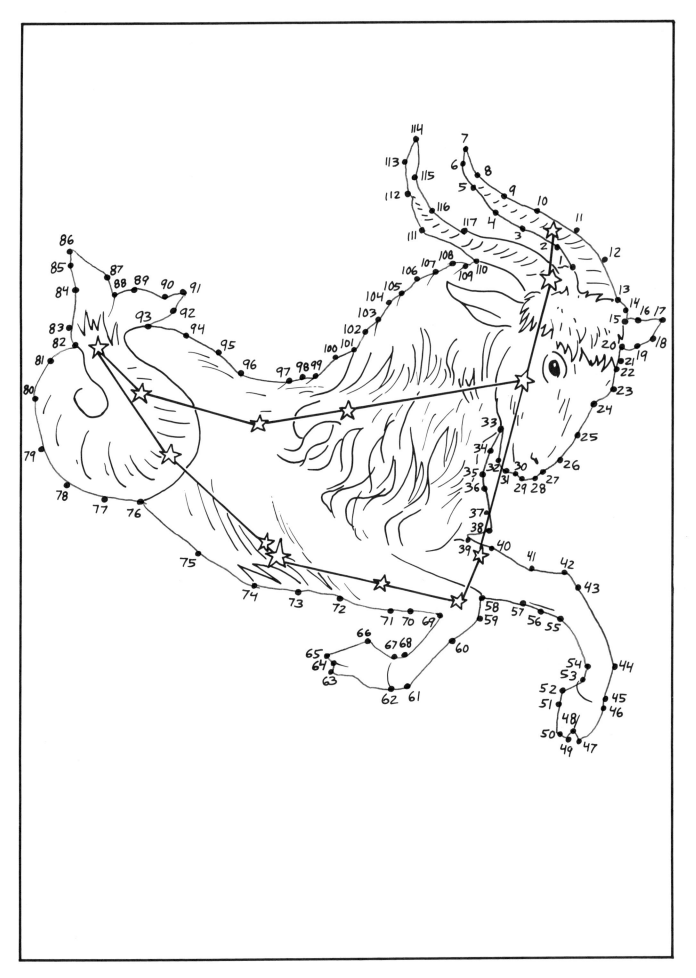

DRACO, THE DRAGON

Legend: There once was a war between the old gods, called the Titans, and the new gods, Zeus and the others who lived on Mount Olympus. The Titans had many monsters on their side. Draco was one of them. After ten years of fighting, Athena, the goddess of wisdom, took the dragon by his tail and tossed him away from the earth. The dragon sailed away, twisting up into many knots until he hit the dome of the stars and froze there.

Number of Stars: 18 (Two are double stars.)

Star Facts: Over thousands of years, Earth wobbles on its axis and stars appear to be in different places in the sky. In our time, the star Polaris helps us figure out which way is north. But 4,000 years ago, Thuban, a star in Draco, was the Pole Star. The Egyptians used it to place the entrances to their pyramids, which all had to face north. In those days, Thuban would shine right down into the pyramid.

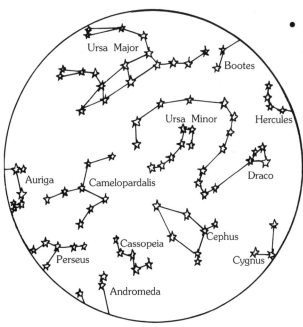

• Arabs saw this constellation as four camels protecting a baby camel from hyenas.

Major Constellations of the Northern Hemisphere

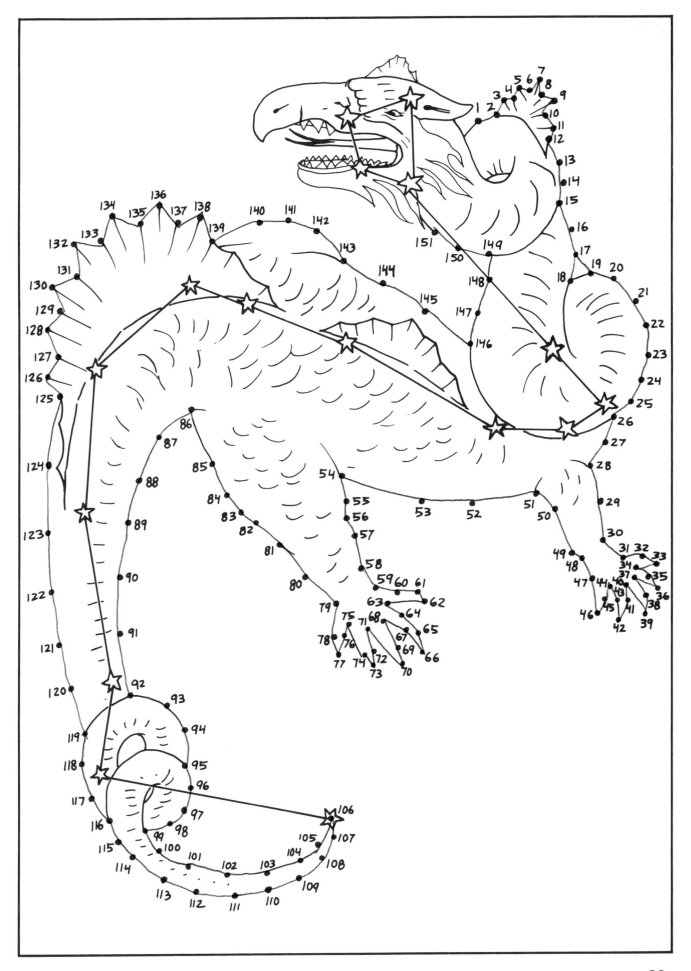

CRUX, THE SOUTHERN CROSS

Legend: The Southern Cross is a modern constellation. It is a symbol of the southern hemisphere and appears on the flags of several countries.

Number of Stars: 5

Special Stars: The beautiful "Jewel Box" is a group of about 50 bright stars in this constellation. Also here is the "Coal Sack," which looks like a dark spot in the Milky Way, but is really a dark cloud of dust and gas.

Star Facts: The Southern Cross is the smallest constellation, but it has helped guide sailors for centuries. Its long arm points south.

Did You Know?   Many stars are only visible from either the North or the South part of the world. The Southern Cross can be seen only from places deep in the Southern hemisphere.

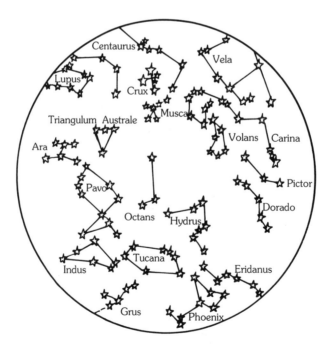

Major Constellations of the Southern Hemisphere

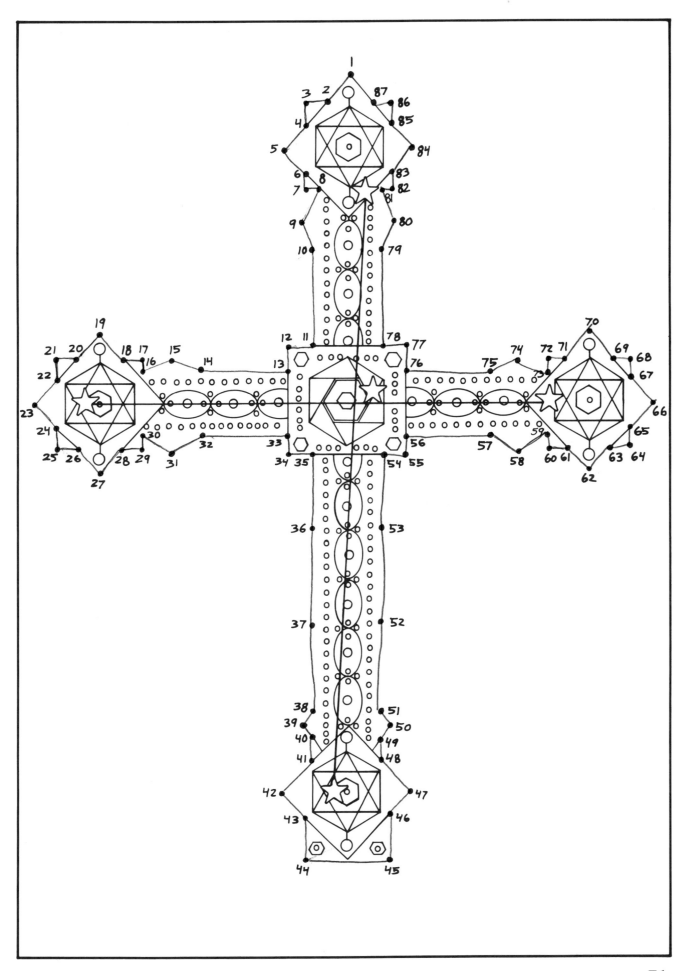

TUCANA, THE TOUCAN

Legend: A toucan is a bird that lives south of the equator. It has a large and brightly colored beak. This constellation was named by Johann Bayer in 1603 in a book he published about the stars. Because Toucan is so close to the celestial south pole, sometimes it looks as if it is flying upside down.

Number of Stars: 6

Special Stars: Toucan seems to sit on top of the Small Magellanic Cloud. This is a giant group of stars called a globular cluster. It looks almost as large as a full moon, but it is very faint. Globular clusters lie outside our Milky Way Galaxy. They contain many very old stars.

Did You Know? Most constellations were named by people long, long ago. However, some parts of the night sky were left out. Sometimes they were left out because there were no bright stars in those spots. Also, there were stars near the celestial south pole that people from the north had never seen. A few hundred years ago, some astronomers made up constellations for these newly seen stars.

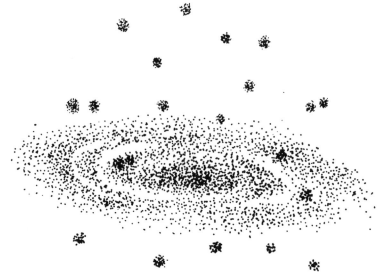

The Small Magellanic Cloud is one of many globular clusters that orbit the Milky Way Galaxy.

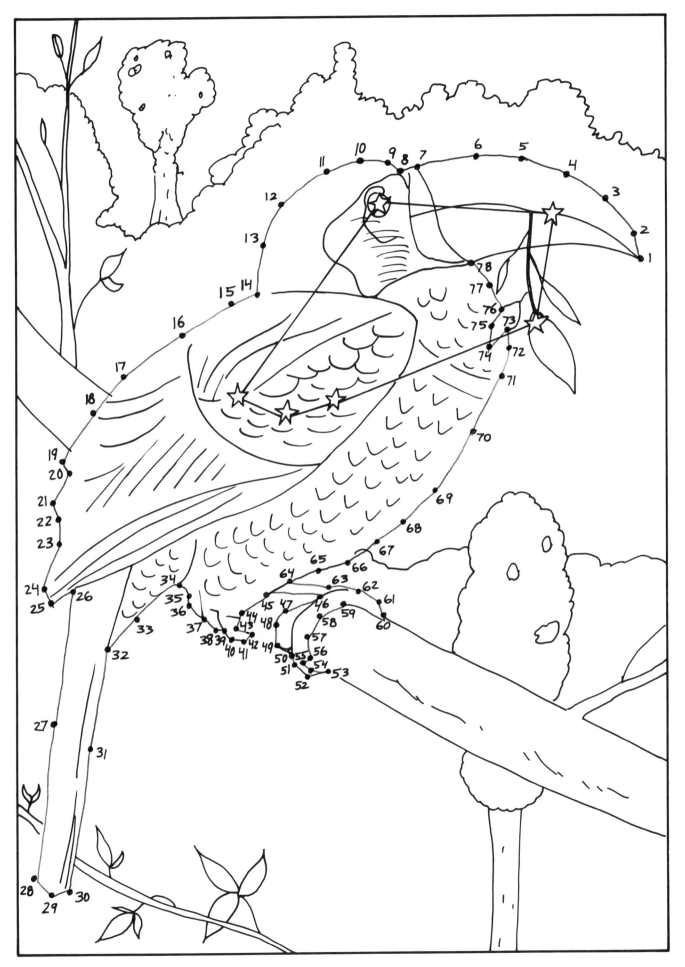

73

DORADO, THE "GOLD" FISH, AND VOLANS, THE FLYING FISH

Legend:
When sailors went down into southern seas, sometimes the Dorado fish (also called pompanos, or mahi-mahi by the Hawaiians) would swim beside their boats. The Dorado is big and has bright skin that turns gold when it dries, so this constellation is called the "Gold" Fish.

Right beside it is the constellation of Volans, the Flying Fish. Flying Fish are also found in the south seas, and have long fins. They jump out of the water, and can soar for short distances. The Dorado follows schools of Flying Fish to catch and eat them. These constellations were created by Johann Bayer in 1603 after he heard stories from the sailors about the fish and the stars south of the Equator.

Number of Stars: Dorado: 5
Volans: 6

Special Stars:
The Large Magellanic Cloud is in Dorado. Like the Small Magellanic Cloud, it is a large group of stars that lies outside our Milky Way Galaxy. In 1987, a star exploded in the Large Magellanic Cloud; it was the first supernova to be seen with modern telescopes.

Some stars end their life in a gigantic explosion called a supernova.

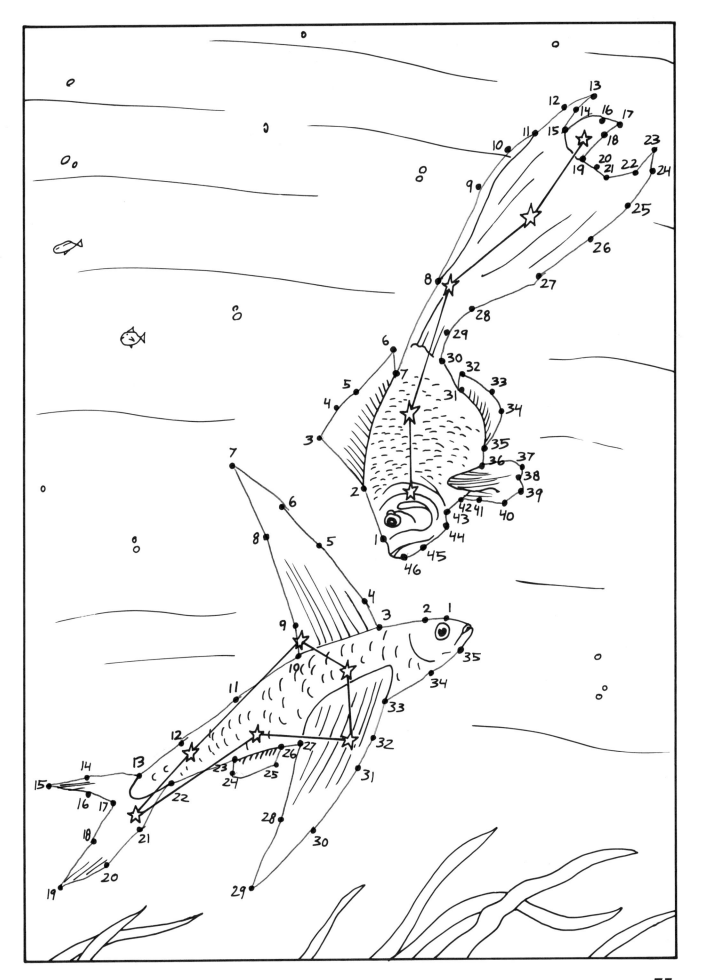

CAMELOPARDALIS, THE GIRAFFE

Legend: This modern constellation was first named Camel, then Camel-Leopard. The Camel-Leopard was a mythical beast with the head of a camel and the spots of a leopard. Nowadays it is seen as a giraffe, which has spots too.

Number of Stars: 10

Special Stars: Though the Giraffe is a big constellation, it has very few bright stars. Many faint stars in this constellations can be seen as the spots of the Giraffe. There are at least two galaxies in this constellation. One of them may be the third closest galaxy to us. It has no name, just a number (IC 342). (IC means "index catalog.")

Did You Know? Galaxies are very large groups of stars. Our Milky Way Galaxy is in a group of galaxies called "The Local Group." It is an incredibly large area of space (four million light-years across!), containing about 24 galaxies. This entire "Local Group" is part of an even larger formation called a supercluster. This vast area contains thousands of galaxies!

Our supercluster of galaxies is just one of an endless number of superclusters.

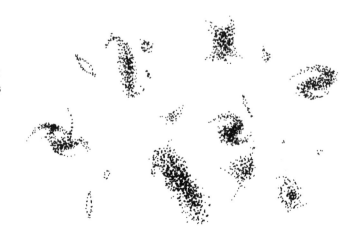

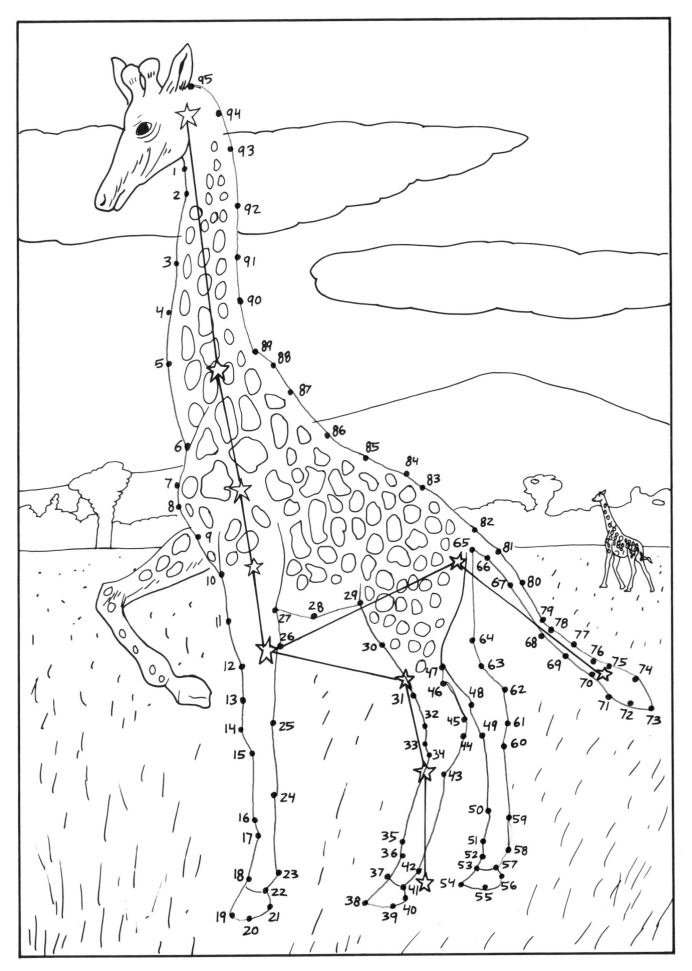

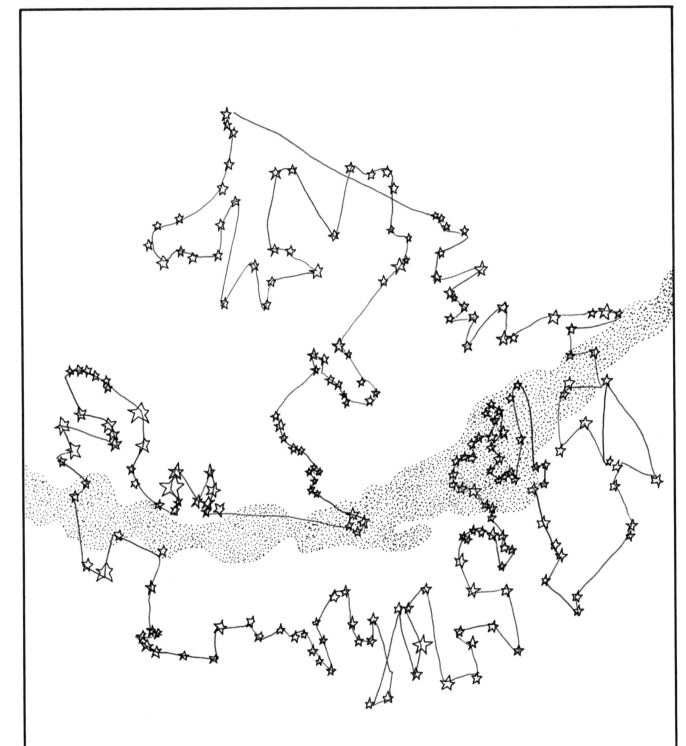

DRAW YOUR OWN CONSTELLATIONS

This is a picture of the entire night sky. All over the world,
people have looked at it and connected the dots of light to form
pictures of characters from stories or objects from their lives.
What do you see when you look at these dots? Can you imagine
your own constellations in the sky?

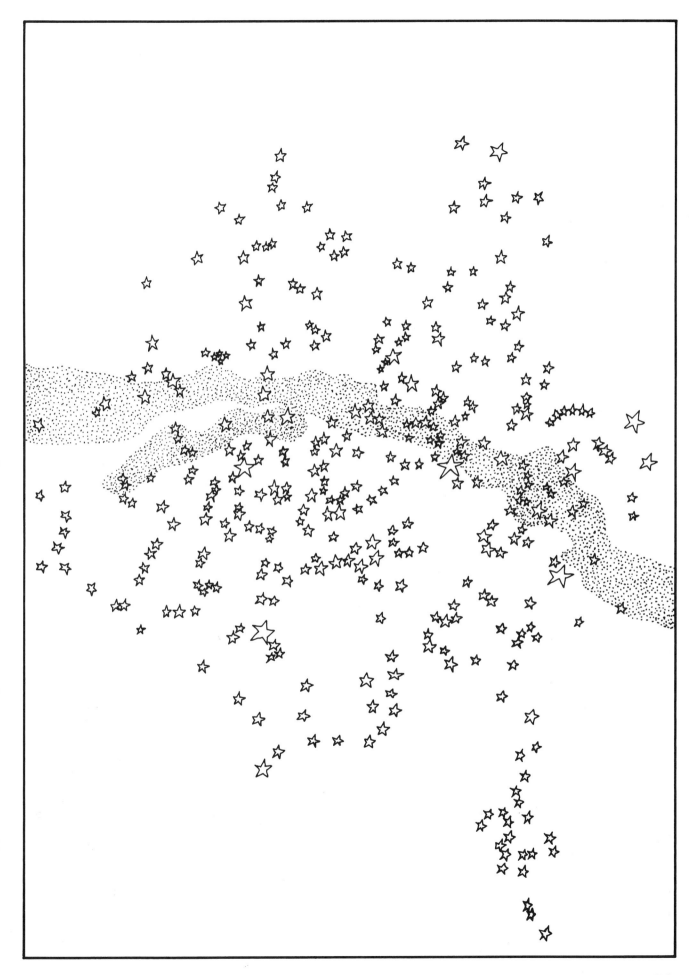

INDEX